P9-DZY-255

THIS
MOMENTOUS
AFFAIR

View of the Presbyterian Meeting House, formerly standing in Federal Street, Boston.

Long Lane Meetinghouse, located on the present site of the Bank of Boston at 100 Federal Street, was the hall to which the delegates moved after other quarters proved inadequate. During the parade that followed the ratification of the Constitution, the people spontaneously declared that Long Lane would henceforth be known as Federal Street.

BOSTON COMMISSION ON THE
BICENTENNIAL OF THE U.S.
CONSTITUTION AND THE
BILL OF RIGHTS

THIS
MOMENTOUS
AFFAIR

*Massachusetts and
the Ratification of the
Constitution of the
United States*

BY
THOMAS H. O'CONNOR
ALAN ROGERS

TRUSTEES OF THE PUBLIC
LIBRARY OF THE CITY OF BOSTON

1987

CREDITS

The National Portrait Gallery, Smithsonian Institution, for woodcut of Gen. Daniel Shays and Col. Job Shattuck

Museum of Fine Arts, Boston, for oil on canvas portraits of Mrs.
James Warren (Mercy Otis), painted in 1763 by John Singleton
Copley (American, 1738-1815), bequeathed to the Museum by
Winslow Warren

Culver Pictures, for view of the Hamilton float bearing the "ship
of state" through the crowds

Boston Athenaeum, for portrait of Nathaniel Gorham and for
View of Presbyterian Meeting House

Boston Public Library

Print Department, for view of Faneuil Hall

Rare Books and Manuscripts Department, for portraits of Caleb
Strong, Rufus King, Elbridge Gerry, Jeremy Belknap, John Hancock, Samuel Adams; two representations of Federal Pillars;
woodcut View of Boston by James Turner Active.

Jane Manthorne, Senior Editor
Jacqueline Whidden, Editor and Researcher
Richard Zonghi, Designer and Production Coordinator
Printed by Thomas Todd Company, Boston

ISBN 0-89073-079-2

Copyright © 1987 Trustees of The Public Library of The
City of Boston

Foreword

IN the following pages you will read of the leadership role played by the City of Boston and the Commonwealth of Massachusetts in providing stable and effective government within the context of the federal system set in motion by our unique constitutional framework.

In their sparking the flame of American liberty, in their service and sacrifice in the American Revolution itself, the men and women of our city and state shared in shaping the federal Constitution as a living document for a free people and in its ratification as a significant one.

In *This Momentous Affair* Boston historians Thomas O'Connor and Alan Rogers, both members of the Boston Commission of the Bicentennial of The U.S. Constitution and The Bill of Rights, have described the historic role played by The Commonwealth and its communities in building a federal union and in laying the foundation for a system of constitutional government that has withstood the test of time.

This book is a valuable and important exercise that should be required reading for young and old alike. For in the pages of this publication, we hear the words of those who debated the ratification of the Constitution, and we see also the origins of the system of government that protects our rights and liberties today.

RAYMOND L. FLYNN
Mayor of Boston

April 2, 1987

Acknowledgments

JUST as the framing and ratification of the Constitution was a cooperative effort among delegates from all over the United States and representatives from towns throughout the Commonwealth of Massachusetts, *This Momentous Affair* is the product of a joint enterprise among a number of local institutions involved with commemorating the bicentennial of the United States Constitution:

Boston College, which offers this volume as its academic contribution to the celebration of the 200th anniversary of the Constitution.

Bank of Boston, then as now an active participant in civic affairs, which has generously supported this historic project.

Office of the Mayor, which provided the stimulus for a volume which would awaken the school children of Boston to the richness of their national heritage.

Boston Bicentennial Commission, which has for members of the greater Boston community renewed the meaning of the phrase, "We, the people."

Boston Public Library, which, in publishing this volume, continues its role as a repository — and a force — for knowledge.

Contents

	Foreword	v
	Acknowledgments	vii
PART I	Massachusetts and the Road to Union	1
	The Mt. Vernon Conference	3
	The Annapolis Convention	3
	Farmers and Debtors	4
	Shays' Rebellion	4
	The Philadelphia Convention	6
	Advocates of Nationalism	6
	Advocates of Local Autonomy	9
	The Ratification Process	11
	The Ratifying Convention	11
PART II	The Struggle for Ratification	14
	Prospects for Ratification	16
	The Federalist Strategy	16
	The Antifederalist Position	17
	Arguments Against Ratification	19
	The Nature of the Government	20
	Hancock's Amendments	20
	Shifting the Balance	23
	The Final Vote	24

Contents

PART III The Ratifying Debates   26

Elections: How Often. Article I, Section 2   26

Elections: Who Regulates. Article I, Section 4   33

Elections: How Many Representatives.
Article I, Section 2   37

The Powers of Congress. Article I, Section 8   39

The Existence of Slavery. Article I, Section 9   49

The Nature of the Judiciary. Article III   50

Hancock's Amendments   55

PART IV The Bay State and the Union   67

Popular Reaction   67

The Grand Procession   68

The Voice of the People   70

The End of the "Old Confederation"   70

Appendices   73

The Constitution of the United States
of America   73

Amendments to the Constitution   88

The Delegates   98

Suggested Reading   111

Index   113

About the Authors   117

PART I

Massachusetts and the Road to Union

FROM 1630, the people of Boston had struggled to build an ordered society in which men were free. The Puritans sought to create a "city on a hill," a beacon to guide a corrupt world. This was Boston's mission.

During the struggle with Great Britain that climaxed in the American Revolution it was Bostonians, steeped in the legacy of Puritan idealism, who articulated a new political ideology called republicanism. In many ways, therefore, the language and goals of American republicanism were a secularized version of the Puritan's attempt to harness man's selfish and individualistic impulses and to create a political community in which men and women were linked to one another in harmony and benevolence.

More than any other form of government, a republic depended upon the virtue of its people. A virtuous citizen worked hard in order to achieve economic independence. But prosperity was not a goal to be chased single-mindedly and selfishly. A virtuous citizen wanted nothing of luxury and extravagance. A good republican focused instead on what would be best for the community. John Warren, the leading doctor and surgeon in post-Revolutionary Boston, summed up the danger confronting republicanism in his Fourth of July oration in 1783. "When virtue fails," Warren told a crowd gathered at the Old State House, "when luxury and corruption shall undermine the pillars of the state," it will cause "a total loss of liberty and patriotism."

Bostonians were obsessed with the radical doctrine of republicanism and committed to a moral crusade to forge a republic of free, selfless individuals. This noble ideal was the engine that powered the Revolution. By the 1780's, however, disillusion had set in. The long, difficult War for Independence, and the eco-

A view of Boston in 1745. In the foreground of this woodcut by James Turner Active, a local mathematician and printer, is an Indian holding a bow in his left hand and a peace-pipe in his right hand; in the background the town of Boston is seen from the harbor, with Long Wharf jutting out into the water and the spires of the meetinghouses and churches rising into the sky.

nomic depression that followed, sapped some people's enthusiasm for liberty and made others impatient to achieve personal prosperity.

Most people simply were not willing to make further sacrifices. After all, Boston was an international port, a town dependent upon trade for its life. Bostonians loved commerce "with its conveniences and pleasures" too much to put up with economic deprivation, observed a worried John Adams. "Will you tell me how to prevent riches from producing luxury?" he asked Thomas Jefferson. "Will you tell me how to prevent wealth from producing an inequality of condition?" The problem was simple: individual wealth, or even the selfish drive for personal gain, undermined political virtue. A truly republican community, therefore, was well-nigh impossible.

Adams knew this problem was not Boston's alone. It was an American dilemma. How was republicanism to be reconciled with individualism? How was political authority to be balanced by personal liberty? This was to be a puzzle that Americans from all parts of the country would struggle with as they made every effort to transform the heady promises of the Revolution into the political realities of a new nation.

The most important problem which faced the United States after it had won its independence in 1783 was the establishment of a stable and effective government. At first, it seemed only natural to most Americans to keep the central government that had successfully held them together during the difficult days of the Revolution and that had led them to ultimate victory — the Articles of Confederation. After several years, however, it was clear that a considerable number of Americans felt that steps should be taken to strengthen the power of the central government and to make other improvements in the Articles. Not that the people wanted to scrap the Articles or do away with the American republican experiment. Far from it! Most Americans were convinced that they were on the right track, and that a political system that put power into the hands of the people was fundamentally correct. But some Americans came to believe that the Articles of Confederation should be made much stronger in order to ensure stability and liberty.

The Mount Vernon Conference

In March 1785 a group of delegates from Maryland and Virginia gathered at Alexandria, Virginia, to work out a satisfactory solution to the problem of navigation rights on Chesapeake Bay and the Potomac River. At the invitation of George Washington, the delegates adjourned to the general's home at Mount Vernon, where their discussions quickly culminated in a settlement concerning the jurisdiction of the Potomac and the apportionment of costs for marking the channel through the Chesapeake Bay. The delegates then drafted a proposal recommending to their respective state legislatures uniform regulations and imposts, and the holding of an annual conference on commercial problems common to them all.

The Annapolis Convention

The legislature of Maryland not only endorsed this proposal but also suggested that both Pennsylvania and Delaware send delegates to the next conference. Agreeing with Maryland's suggestion, the legislature of Virginia called for all thirteen states to send representatives to a convention to be held at Annapolis, Maryland, in September 1786 to discuss commercial problems. This new convention, however, drew delegates from only five states – Delaware, New Jersey, New York, Pennsylvania, and Virginia. Although the twelve delegates present were disappointed by the meager turnout, they followed the suggestion of Alexander Hamilton of New York and adopted a resolution asking Congress to call upon the states to send delegates to a new convention to be held on the second Monday in May 1787, "for the sole and express purpose of revising the Articles of Confederation." Congress cautiously endorsed this resolution and called for the convention to convene in Philadelphia as proposed. Delegates were chosen by the legislature of every state except Rhode Island, and proceeded to the convention site to take part in one of the most momentous gatherings in history.

Farmers and Debtors

One reason why so many people agreed to support the move to revise the Articles of Confederation and strengthen the central government was the growing anxiety in many parts of the country over the troubled state of the economy. After the Revolution had ended, a period of deflation forced down prices and greatly reduced personal incomes. People who had purchased goods, livestock, and farmlands when times were good and money plentiful now found themselves in serious economic trouble. The number of mortgage foreclosures and business failures rose to new heights, and many people were actually put into prison for failure to pay their debts.

Shays' Rebellion

In Massachusetts the problem of deflation was particularly acute. With overseas markets closed by the British, and with consumers at home holding tight to whatever cash they had left, a chain of debt stretched from Boston to Worcester, to the subsistence farmers who lived on the small farms of western Massachusetts. Instead of issuing paper money to alleviate the problem, however, the state legislature ignored the farmers' protests and proceeded to levy new and heavier taxes in an attempt to pay off the war debt. This action proved too much for the hard-pressed farmers. Because their petitions to the General Court calling for reform were ignored, they organized county conventions to hammer out alternative programs and to gather support for their cause. When their efforts failed, farmers and laborers who had lost confidence in the government's ability or willingness to help them, moved to block or "regulate" the courts. They had no intention of overthrowing the Commonwealth, and they were rarely violent, but by barring the courts from sitting, these desperate farmers effectively prevented the fulfillment of contracts and the collection of back taxes. By the summer of 1786, mob action had broken out as bands of insurgents marched on various courts throughout the western sections of the state, and prevented them from sitting to hear cases.

In an attempt to smash the growing rebellion, as well as to protect the members of the state's Supreme Court which was sitting at Springfield, Governor James Bowdoin called out a force of militiamen under the command of General William

An early woodcut showing Daniel Shays and Job Shattuck, leaders of an uprising of indebted farmers in western Massachusetts who fought to keep the courts from meeting and foreclosing on their mortgages. Shays' Rebellion caused many persons to join the movement to strengthen the central government.

Shepherd. In the meantime, however, a force of some 500 insurgents under the leadership of Daniel Shays, a hard-pressed farmer and former captain of the Revolutionary Army, gathered at Springfield and forced the Supreme Court to adjourn. This action, coupled with the rumor that Shays would move against the courts in Worcester and then seize the national arsenal in Springfield, prompted Governor Bowdoin to reinforce the militia with a force of 4,400 troops under the command of General Benjamin Lincoln. By March of 1787 the uprising was completely crushed, with most of the insurgents, including Captain Shays, under arrest and the remainder of the rebels fleeing into the hills of Vermont.

The Philadelphia Convention

Although Shays' Rebellion was put down, it had important repercussions throughout the Commonwealth and the nation. This insurrection, along with the fear of similar disorders among farmers and debtors in other parts of the country, had come as a frightening shock to the propertied classes and the well-to-do interests. This was the type of "blood anarchy" they greatly feared, and it made the delegates to the upcoming convention in Philadelphia determined that no more such insurrections would take place in the future. It was only a few months later that the convention in Philadelphia opened on May 25, 1787, after a sufficient number of delegates had arrived to form a quorum. Attending the meeting were 55 delegates elected by the legislatures of 12 states, with only Rhode Island still refusing to send any representatives.

Advocates of Nationalism

In many ways the four delegates from the Commonwealth of Massachusetts personified the social and economic attitudes that still divided the Bay State. Two members clearly supported the movement toward a stronger and more centralized government. They felt that such a government would be better able to maintain law and order, to stimulate a prosperous national economy, and to protect the American republic in a world dominated by aggressive monarchies. As a wealthy businessman and the most recent president of the Continental Congress, Nathaniel Gor-

Nathaniel Gorham was born at Charlestown, Massachusetts, and after a period of apprenticeship became successful in his own business while still a young man. He became a prominent member of the Massachusetts General Court, served as speaker of the Massachusetts House, and after the Revolution was elected President of the Continental Congress. At the Philadelphia Convention his was a persuasive voice for the business and commercial interests of the nation, calling for a strong and active central government.

ham enjoyed considerable prestige among the other delegates at the convention, and was a persuasive spokesman for the mercantile interests of the whole New England region. His colleague, thirty-two-year-old Rufus King, was one of the youngest and most articulate speakers. He argued that the new govern-

H B Hall.

Rufus King was born at Scarborough, Maine, the son of a wealthy merchant. After graduating from Harvard, he studied law at Newburyport and then entered the General Court of Massachusetts. At the age of 32, King was one of the youngest delegates at the Philadelphia Convention where he was a strong supporter of the large states and the Virginia plan. After serving as a member of the Massachusetts ratifying convention, he went on to serve as Senator from New York from 1789 to 1796 and from 1813 to 1825, after which he became United States Minister to Great Britain.

ment had to be founded on economic interests and made attractive to able and ambitious men, or else unchecked human passions would bring about anarchy and ruin. Both these delegates steadfastly argued in favor of a stronger central government for the nation and called for a vigorous and independent chief executive.

An attorney in Hampshire County, Caleb Strong was an officer of the court closed by the Shays' rebels, and later helped collect their surrendered weapons. At the Philadelphia Convention, he joined with Elbridge Gerry to divide Massachusetts on the Connecticut Compromise vote, thus weakening the unity of the larger states and making a final compromise possible. Strong later served as Governor of Massachusetts from 1800 to 1807, and from 1812 to 1816.

Advocates of Local Autonomy

The other two members, however, were much more protective of states' rights and local autonomy. Caleb Strong, an experienced lawyer and politician from Northampton who had helped draft the Massachusetts Constitution of 1780, was more cautious in his approach. While he supported the idea of a stronger cen-

Elbridge Gerry was born and raised in Marblehead, Massachusetts, the third of twelve children in a mercantile family. Following graduation from Harvard College, he joined his father and brothers in exporting dried fish to Europe and the West Indies. After serving in the General Court, he attended the Philadelphia Convention where he spoke out in favor of state sovereignty. While he warned against giving excessive power and authority to the central government, he also expressed fears about too much democracy in local populations. Gerry refused to sign the Constitution, and opposed ratification when he returned to Massachusetts.

tral government, he argued in favor of checks and balances that would restrict the powers of that government. He would let the states pay the salaries of Congress, and he recommended annual elections for the House of Representatives. Although Strong had to leave Philadelphia early, he publicly supported the new Constitution when it arrived in Massachusetts. The fourth member of the Bay State delegation, and the man who voiced the strongest opposition views was Elbridge Gerry from Marblehead. Gerry agreed that the new government should have increased commercial powers to raise the revenue, pay off the debt, and negotiate commercial treaties, but he was strongly opposed to allowing such a government to exercise any political controls over state governments or local concerns. Fearing that the convention had created too strong a chief executive and had extended the federal court system too far, Gerry refused to sign the final document when it was completed. He expressed the fear that those people of Massachusetts who were "devoted to democracy" would start a civil war in opposition to the new Constitution.

The Ratification Process

At the end of seventeen long, hot, and steamy weeks – from May 25 to September 17, 1787 – only 41 of the original 55 delegates still remained in Philadelphia to put their signatures on the new Constitution of the United States. Three members, including Governor Edmund Randolph and George Mason of Virginia, and Elbridge Gerry of Massachusetts, had declined to do so on the grounds that the Constitution did not include a Bill of Rights, and had returned to their respective states to fight ratification. At the first session of the General Court of Massachusetts during his second administration, Governor John Hancock ordered Secretary John Avery to lay "this momentous affair" before the legislators, and made a noncommital speech calling attention to the "truly respectable" character of the men who had framed the document in Philadelphia. It was then decided to have the Commonwealth act upon the proposed Constitution at a convention which would open at Boston in January. A special election was held in each of the towns to select delegates to the ratifying convention. Candidates – Federalists or Antifederalists – were chosen on the basis of their pledges for or against the Constitution.

The Ratifying Convention

The opening session of the Massachusetts ratifying convention was held on January 8, 1788. A total of 364 delegates from across

The Rev. Jeremy Belknap came to Boston from New Hampshire early in 1787. An author, historian, and founder of the Massachusetts Historical Society, Belknap recorded valuable thumbnail sketches of many delegates at the ratifying convention.

the Commonwealth — the largest convention called in any state — jammed into the Old State House. The following day the members moved to the Brattle Street Church where the Hancock family had owned a pew for more than a century. Dissatisfied with the poor acoustics in the spacious building, however, they briefly moved back to the Old State House and then, on January 17, settled down in Dr. Jeremy Belknap's house of worship on Long Lane.

The delegation from Boston consisted of seventeen members. This number included two from Roxbury, two from Dorchester, and one from Charlestown — all of which were then separate communities. The Boston delegation was talented and remarkable, if for no other reason than it marked the first time in the town's long and tumultuous political history that the North End and South End caucuses agreed to cooperate. Governor John Hancock had been selected as a representative of the town itself, but so too had his political rival, former governor James Bowdoin. Also included in the Boston delegation was Sam Adams, the popular revolutionary hero, who quietly let it be known that he had serious reservations about the proposed constitution.

It was apparent as soon as the debates began that the delegates were conscious that they were involved in a historic undertaking. Massachusetts was the second most populous state in the Union at that time and certainly one of the most influential. If the new framework of government failed to be ratified in the Bay State, then the entire movement to create a new national government might well collapse. The future of the Union was in the balance as the delegates debated the relative merits of the Constitution of the United States.

PART II

The Struggle for Ratification

IN late September 1787, the proposed Constitution was published in Boston. Mercy Otis Warren, an ardent patriot, essayist, and historian, described its initial reception to an English friend:

> It is now only three days since the publication of the recommendations of this respectable body has appeared in our papers; almost everyone whom I have yet seen reads with attention, folds the paper with solemnity and silently wraps up his opinions within his own breast, as if afraid of interrupting the calm expectation that has prevailed all ranks for several months apart.

By January 1788 when the Massachusetts ratifying convention officially began to discuss the Constitution, the scene of quiet contemplation recorded by Mrs. Warren was replaced by a vociferous political debate. While one prominent Federalist boasted that "adoption will be easy," more realistic analysts pointed out that there were at least three groups which would offer serious opposition to the proposed Constitution. First, many of the Old Revolutionary activists attacked the Constitution as a vehicle for "the hideous demon of Aristocracy," the very enemy independence from Great Britain was to have eliminated from American politics. Mrs. Warren, among others, sided with this group, arguing that the new frame of government did not protect American virtue from the dangers of restless ambition and selfishness. A second faction opposed to ratification was composed of those men from western Massachusetts who were allied, either intellectually or actually, with Shays' Rebellion. Western farmers believed that, like the state government against which they had rebelled in 1786, the new national government would favor the commercial interests to the detriment of family farmers. Delegates from the district of Maine formed a third

Mercy Otis Warren was a member of the prominent Otis family from Barnstable, and wife of James Warren. An intellectual figure in her own right, she had written privately and publicly about politics for more than twenty years when, in 1788, she published "Observations on the New Constitution." Although Warren's Antifederalism had softened by 1805, when she published a three-volume history of the American Revolution, she outraged John Adams by charging that he had forgotten "the principles of the Revolution." She died in 1813 at the age of 86.

group of Antifederalists who had announced their opposition to the Constitution before the convention began. They already had decided to vote against ratification because they were convinced that the Constitution would make it more difficult for Maine to separate from Massachusetts. When the "honest, doubting people" were added to these groups, one delegate observed, the Antifederalists made "a powerful host."

Prospects for Ratification

By the time the convention began, therefore, the Federalists' early optimism had faded. Rufus King, who had participated in creating the new Constitution and in 1788 was a delegate from Newburyport to the ratifying convention, told James Madison, "I am pretty well satisfied we shall lose the question." And, "on the opening of the convention," General Henry Knox complained to George Washington that "a majority were prejudiced against the Constitution."

Still, if the Federalists seemed to be outnumbered, they had enlisted a glittering array of the Bay State's most prominent men in their cause. Of the 364 delegates elected by the people to debate the merits of the Constitution, most of the wealth and talent were in favor of ratification. One historian has estimated that 87% of the merchants and 77% of the professionals who were delegates voted for the Constitution, as did 75% of those delegates who owned government bonds.

The Federalist Strategy

To make their case the Federalists relied upon a cluster of well prepared, articulate, experienced debaters. Nathaniel Gorham, one of two delegates from Massachusetts to sign the Constitution in Philadelphia (King was the other), boasted to James Madison that among the Federalist delegates were "three judges of the supreme court, fifteen members of the Senate, twenty from among the most respectable of the clergy, ten or twelve of the first characters at the bar, judges of probate, high sheriffs of counties and three generals of the Continental Army." A small leadership cadre drawn from this impressive group worked out the Federalists' convention strategy.

First, the Federalists sought to prolong the convention as long as possible so that they would have ample opportunity to use their superior debating skills to win over the undecided delegates. To achieve this goal, the Federalists insisted upon, and won, the right to discuss each and every clause in the proposed Constitution. The Federalists won another key procedural point which effectively masked their relative lack of strength and greatly improved their chances of success; specifically, a majority of the delegates were convinced by Federalist partisans that there should be no votes taken on particular issues. Rather, the whole document was to be voted up or down at the conclusion of the convention. These two procedural victories had the effect of helping the Federalists meet the "objections that are in the minds of the people" outside the convention. One Federalist, for example, noted with delight that "there are a vast many people attending in the galleries . . . and most of the arguments are published in the papers."

The conclusion to be drawn from an analysis of the strategy used by the Federalists seems unmistakable: far from thinking or acting as an arrogant, disdainful elite, the Federalists who served as delegates in the Massachusetts ratifying convention firmly believed in the reasonableness, "the genius" of the people. They were not democrats, however; for although they believed that the ultimate power of government must reside in the people and that they must have a voice in making all laws, the Federalists feared that the people were too easily "intoxicated with large draughts of liberty. . . ." Shays' Rebellion had proved the validity of this belief. Therefore, Federalists were forced to confront a dilemma perhaps best expressed by the Reverend Jeremy Belknap, in whose church the convention met. How, he asked a friend, might "the principle that government originates from the people" be reconciled with the fact "that they are not able to govern themselves?" The proposed Constitution was the answer, according to Federalists; it would "take up the reins of government" without being "destructive to the liberties of the people."

The Antifederalist Position

The Antifederalists vehemently disagreed. First of all, they were not ready to admit that the current economic and political circumstances were so bad that a new government was necessary. James Winthrop, a librarian at Harvard College, was the first in Massachusetts to attack the Federalists' assertion that immediate, drastic steps needed to be taken. In a series of articles published in the *Massachusetts Gazette* in the winter of 1787-1788, Winthrop produced a long list of the "principal advantages of the happy form of government under which it is our good fortune to live. . . ." There is "every symptom of strength and none of decay," he concluded in his argument to retain the Articles of Confederation.

"Agrippa," the penname used by Winthrop, also argued with force and clarity the common Antifederalist belief that republican government could not operate over a large and heterogeneous nation. "It is impossible," he wrote, "for one code of laws to suit Georgia and Massachusetts." But the new Constitution attempted to do just that by giving Congress new and more sweeping powers. The result, Agrippa warned the delegates to the ratifying convention, will be "a government possessed of much more extensive powers than the present, and subject to much smaller checks." In particular, Agrippa and the Antifederalist delegates worried that without a bill of rights which explicitly protected the liberties of the people, the new government would succumb to the natural temptation "to use power wantonly." As one of the leading Antifederalist spokesmen at the convention put it: "our rulers ought never to have a power which they could abuse."

The powerful and familiar theoretical arguments made by the Antifederalists, however, had to be expressed during the convention by inexperienced delegates. Neither Winthrop nor Elbridge Gerry, who had helped draft the new Constitution but had refused to sign it, were elected to the Massachusetts convention. However, because the Federalists were anxious to appear open and moderate, Gerry was invited "to take a seat in the house to answer any question of *facts* . . . that the Convention may want to ask respecting the passing of the Constitution." Gerry accepted, but soon discovered that speaking only when spoken to was a "humiliating condition" and he asked to be allowed to inform the convention by letter of his *opinion* of the Constitution. While this question was being debated, Gerry angrily began his letter. "He writes, then strikes out, writes on, strikes out again," sarcastically noted "A Spectator." "Were all the debates to be suspended until Mr. E. Gerry had finished his very important letter?" asked the *Centinel*. Certainly not, answered the delegates. Although Gerry's letter eventually was accepted, both he and it were ignored. In one clever move, the Federalists had rendered ineffectual the Antifederalists' most powerful spokesman.

Arguments Against Ratification

In the absence of Gerry, therefore, other less well known Antifederalists carried the fight against ratification. Although they came chiefly from the frontier areas of the Commonwealth, the leaders of the opposition were not poor farmers. William Wedgery owned and built ships in New Gloucester, Maine; Samuel Nasson, of Sanford, Maine, also owned ships and practiced law; and William Thompson from Scarborough, Maine owned more government bonds than all but five of the delegates at the convention. Two of the Antifederalist leaders came from western Massachusetts, Dr. John Taylor from Douglas and Amos Singletary from Sutton. The latter owned a grist mill and had been an enthusiastic supporter of Shays' uprising. Dr. Taylor had served in the Massachusetts House, where he championed a bill to extend the law making paper currency legal tender, a favorite western remedy for economic ills. Jeremy Belknap characterized Taylor's performance during the debates over the Constitution as "cunning . . . but more decent" than Wedgery, Thompson, and Nasson.

Although these Antifederalists were capable and sincere, their rhetorical skills were no match for the more learned Federalist speakers. And they knew it. Nasson, for example, had decided not to run for re-election to the Massachusetts General Court in 1787 because he felt "the want of a proper Education. I feel my self so small on many occasions," Nasson confided to a friend, "that I almost shrunk [sic] into nothing." Amos Singletary also felt the sting of Federalist arrogance. But unlike Nasson, Singletary got angry. He demanded that the Federalists "would not play round the subject with their fine stories, like a fox round a trap, but come to it." Singletary was suspicious. "These lawyers, and men of learning, and monied men that talk so finely and gloss over matters so smoothly to make us poor illiterate people swallow down the pill," he said during the debate over the Constitution, "expect to get into Congress themselves; they expect to be the managers of this Constitution and get all the power and all the money into their own hands; and then they will swallow up all us little folks, like the great *Leviathan* . . . yes, just as the whale swallowed *Jonah*."

The Nature of the Government

Not surprisingly, the different attitudes and ideological perspectives which the Antifederalists and the Federalists brought to the convention caused the delegates to disagree over what kind of government the proposed Constitution would bring into being. Federalists argued that the Constitution was a frame for an energetic government with power enough to make republicanism possible. The Antifederalists saw the Constitution as the means of creating an all-powerful centralized government that would allow an elite to strip away the people's liberty and destroy the republican experiment launched by the Revolution.

Still, too much should not be made of the split between Federalists and Antifederalists. The Reverend Belknap certainly was correct when he said that "men of all professions, of all ranks, and of all characters, good, bad, and indifferent" could be found in both camps. And, most importantly, all the delegates were republicans, men who dreamed of a prosperous independent nation in which the liberties of the people would be protected by the people.

Hancock's Amendments

It was this sentiment to which Governor John Hancock appealed on January 31 when he recommended a series of amendments, "a conciliatory proposition" designed to bridge the gap between Antifederalists and Federalists. Or, as Hancock put it hopefully, the amendments would "remove the fears and quiet the apprehensions of many of the good people of this Commonwealth and more effectually guard against an undue administration of the federal government."

The changes suggested by Hancock were not sweeping. The most important called for powers not expressly delegated to the

John Hancock spent his fortune to help win America's independence and to launch the new government. Signer of the Declaration of Independence, President of the Continental Congress, and nine times governor of Massachusetts, Hancock offered the conciliatory amendments which made ratification possible. He died at the age of 56 practically penniless.

national government to be reserved to the states; another prohibited U.S. citizens from accepting titles or offices from foreign governments; a third stipulated that direct taxes might be enacted only when other sources of revenue proved inadequate; and another that Congress would be allowed to regulate elections only when the state had neglected to do so. Nor did Hancock's recommendations mean that he advocated "conditional" acceptance, as the Antifederalists did. The nine amendments, he explained in his brief speech, were to be recommended to Congress only after the Constitution had been ratified.

M.ʳ SAMUEL ADAMS.

Sam Adams, "the old patriot," had dedicated his life to creating an American republic. Although he was not chosen to attend the Philadelphia Convention, his support of Governor Hancock's amendments at the ratifying convention helped persuade enough delegates to vote in favor of ratification. Defeated for Congress in 1788, he was elected lieutenant-governor in 1789, and capped his long career of public service by serving as governor of the Commonwealth from 1794 to 1797.

Samuel Adams, who had taken little part in the convention to this point, now asked to be heard. For the first time in years, Adams spoke in support of the governor. Hancock's suggested amendments, Adams stated, "will have a tendency to remove . . . doubts and to conciliate the minds of the Convention and the people without doors." Adams sincerely believed that if Massachusetts refused to ratify the Constitution, other states would follow suit; and Antifederalist minorities in those states that had approved the Constitution already would be encouraged. "I fear the consequences of such disunion," the old patriot told the delegates.

Shifting the Balance

Hancock's amendments and Adams' speech dramatically shifted the balance within the convention. The Antifederalists sensed the change and moved to adjourn, hoping to forestall a vote which they now believed the Federalists would carry. But the Federalists, joined by scores of undecided delegates, easily turned back the motion by a vote of 214 to 115.

James Bowdoin, Jr., a Federalist delegate from Dorchester, began the final round of debates. In a long speech studded with references to enlightenment figures and to ancient history, he rehearsed the arguments in favor of the Constitution with a passion which for the first time in a month seemed to be motivated by the belief that victory was possible. Another Boston Federalist, Dr. Charles Jarvis, aggressively argued against the charge that Hancock had introduced amendments merely "to lead to a decision which would otherwise not be had." Nonsense. "Would gentlemen who are opposed to the Constitution wish to have no amendments?" asked Jarvis; "or are they afraid . . . that these propositions will secure a larger majority?"

The Antifederalists fought back weakly. Although Hancock's amendments did go far toward meeting the objections to the Constitution that had been raised, there was no guarantee they would be adopted, said Dr. John Taylor. Added Nathaniel Barrell, a "plain husbandman" from York, Maine, "this is not . . . the most perfect system I could wish." Yet he added, "I think this Constitution, with all its imperfections is excellent compared . . . to the fatal effects of anarchy." Barrell "wished" the convention could be adjourned so that he might consult his constituents. But he knew that was futile, given the recent overwhelming vote against an adjournment. "I am almost tempted," he concluded, "to risk their displeasure and adopt it without their consent."

A turning point had been reached. Barrell's speech was a hint that the Antifederalists' opposition was crumbling. Charles Turner of Scituate delivered the hammer blow. "I have been adverse to the reception of this Constitution while it was considered in its original form," he said. But when the convention approved the amendments introduced by Governor Hancock, Turner abandoned Antifederalism. "I find myself constrained to say, before this Assembly and before God," announced Turner, "that I think it is my duty to give my vote in favor of this Constitution, with the proposed amendments."

The Final Vote

Late on the afternoon of February 6, 1788 the "grand question" was posed. Should Massachusetts ratify the Constitution? The vote was 187 yes, 168 no. By the narrow margin of 19 votes, Massachusetts became the sixth state to join the new union.

Immediately following the vote, Antifederalists were on their feet to pledge their support for the new Constitution. Abraham White, a delegate from Norton, was the first to speak. Although he had opposed the Constitution, White said he now intended "to induce his constituents to live in peace under, and cheerfully submit to it." Wedgery, one of the Antifederalists' most outspoken leaders, made the same pledge. Moreover, he told the convention that he would work against continuing any "measure of a protest." Finally, he thanked the people of Boston "for the civility which [they] have shown to the convention." Wedgery's statement was more than political politeness. Two days after the vote, he praised Bostonians again. "Notwithstanding my opposition to the Constitution and the anxiety of Boston for its adoption," Wedgery wrote a friend, "I must tell you I was never treated with so much politeness in my Life as I was afterwards by the tradesmen of Boston, merchants and every other gentleman."

THE FEDERAL PILLARS.

UNITED THEY STAND—DIVIDED FALL.

BOSTON, *Friday, February 8.*

FEDERAL PILLARS.

Ratification of the Federal Constitution by
Maſſachuſetts.

The upper drawing appeared in the *Massachusetts Centinel* on January 16, 1788, a week after the ratifying convention had begun its deliberations. It dramatizes the fear of many people, that if Massachusetts failed to ratify the Constitution, there would not be enough support to sustain a strong, unified government.

The lower drawing appeared in the *Massachusetts Gazette* on February 8, 1788, the day after the news had been announced that Massachusetts had ratified the Constitution. As the sixth state to ratify the new document, Massachusetts has obviously become a strong pillar of the new government, and an inducement for other states to follow suit.

PART III

The Ratifying Debates*

IN the course of the Massachusetts ratifying convention, several key constitutional issues became the subject of heated debate among the delegates. The lengthiest and most important debate came over Article I, section 2, which stipulated that representatives to the United States Congress would serve a two-year term. ("Oh, my country," exclaimed General Samuel Thompson, "never give up your annual elections; young men never give up your jewel.") The powers that were to be exercised by Congress (Article I, section 8) also stimulated an acrimonious controversy. Likewise, the role of the federal judiciary (Article III) came under sharp attack from Antifederalists. Finally, while no one actually defended the institution of slavery, delegates differed over whether the proposed Constitution would prolong or shorten the life of that "peculiar institution" as time went on. The selections from the debates which follow highlight the key differences between Federalists and Antifederalists as they debated these issues at the convention.

Elections: How Often?
ARTICLE I, SECTION 2

The debate over the ratification of the Constitution of the United States began with Article I, section 2. Antifederalists strongly believed annual elections to the House of Representatives were an essential part of a republican government. Speeches by John Taylor from Douglas, Massachusetts, and General Samuel Thompson, a delegate from Maine, took as their starting point the Antifederalists' favorite political

*Text of the debates has been selected from "Report of the Debates of the Convention of 1788" in *Debates and Proceedings in the Convention of the Commonwealth of Massachusetts, held in the year 1788, and which finally ratified the Constitution of the United States*. Boston, William White, 1856.

*maxim: "where annual elections end, tyranny begins." The Federalists
— Fisher Ames, James Bowdoin, John Brooks, and Christopher Gore
— countered by arguing that a two-year term would help create the
stability necessary to the preservation of liberty.*

Taylor spoke first.

Mr. President, I am opposed to biennial, and am in favor of
annual elections. Annual elections have been the practice of this
State ever since its settlement, and no objection to such a mode
of electing has ever been made. It has, indeed, Sir, been considered as the safeguard of the liberties of the people; and the
annihilation of it, the avenue through which tyranny will enter.
By the articles of confederation, annual elections are provided
for, though we have additional securities in a right to recall any,
or all of our members from Congress, and a provision for rotation. In the proposed Constitution there is no provision for rotation; we have no right by it to recall our delegates. In answer
to the observation, that, by frequency of elections, good men
will be excluded, I answer, if they behave well, it is probable
they will be continued; but if they behave ill, how shall we remedy the evil? It is possible that rulers may be appointed who
may wish to root out the liberties of the people. Is it not, Mr.
President, better, if such a case should occur, that at a short
period they should politically die, than that they should be proceeded against by impeachment? These considerations, and others, said the Doctor, make me in favor of annual elections; and
the further we deviate therefrom, the greater is the evil.

*Young Fisher Ames from Dedham was one of the Federalists' most
brilliant and powerful speakers. He later served in the U.S. House of
Representatives from 1789-1797.*

Biennial elections appear to me, Sir, an essential security to
liberty. These are my reasons: —

Faction and enthusiasm are the instruments by which popular
governments are destroyed. We need not talk of the power of
an aristocracy. The people, when they lose their liberties, are
cheated out of them. They nourish factions in their bosoms,
which will subsist so long as abusing their honest credulity shall
be the means of acquiring power. A democracy is a volcano,
which conceals the fiery means of its own destruction. These

will produce an eruption, and carry desolation in their way. The people always mean right, and if time is allowed for reflection and information, they will do right. I would not have the first wish, the momentary impulse of the public mind, become law. For it is not always the sense of the people, with whom I admit that all power resides. On great questions, we first hear the loud clamors of passion, artifice and faction. I consider biennial elections as a security that the sober second thought of the people shall be law. There is a calm review of public transactions, which is made by the citizens who have families and children, the pledges of their fidelity. To provide for popular liberty, we must take care that measures shall not be adopted without due deliberation. The member chosen for two years will feel some independence in his seat. The factions of the day will expire before the end of the term.

The people will be proportionally attentive to the merits of a candidate. Two years will afford opportunity to the member to deserve well of them, and they will require evidence that he has done it.

But, Sir, the representatives are the grand inquisition of the Union. They are, by impeachment, to bring great offenders to justice. One year will not suffice to detect guilt, and to pursue it to conviction; therefore, they will escape, and the balance of the two branches will be destroyed, and the people oppressed with impunity. The senators will represent the sovereignty of the States. The representatives are to represent the people. The offices ought to bear some proportion in point of importance. This will be impossible if they are chosen for one year only.

Will the people then blind the eyes of their own watchmen? Will they bind the hands which are to hold the sword for their defence? Will they impair their own power, by an unreasonable jealousy of themselves?

For these reasons, I am clearly of opinion that the article is entitled to our approbation as it stands; and as it has been demanded, why annual elections were not preferred to biennial, permit me to retort the question, and to inquire, in my turn, what reason can be given, why, if annual elections are good, biennial elections are not better?

James Bowdoin had been governor of the Commonwealth during that

tumultuous year when the western counties rose in rebellion. His re-
fusal to compromise with the Shaysites and his heavy-handed use of
military force led the voters to push him aside in 1787. Hancock was
reelected governor by a better-than-3-to-1 margin. According to Fed-
eralist strategy, Bowdoin adopted a moderate tone during the conven-
tion.

The Hon. Mr. Bowdoin remarked on the idea suggested by
the honorable gentleman from Scituate, [Mr. Turner,] who had
said that nature pointed out the propriety of *annual* elections,
by its *annual* renewal, and observed, that if the revolution of the
heavenly bodies is to be the principle to regulate elections, it
was not fixed to any period; as in some of the systems it would
be very short; and in the last discovered planet it would be
eighty of our years. Gentlemen, he said, who had gone before
him in the debate, had clearly pointed out the alteration of the
election of our federal representatives, from annual to biennial,
to be justifiable. Annual elections may be necessary in this State;
but in the choice of representatives for the continent, it ought
to be longer; nor did he see any danger in its being so. Who,
he asked, are the men to be elected? Are they not to be from
among us? If they were to be a distinct body, then the doctrine
of precaution, which gentlemen use, would be necessary. But,
Sir, they can make no laws, nor levy any taxes, but those to
which they themselves must be subservient — they themselves
must bear a part; therefore, our security is guaranteed, by their
being thus subject to the laws, if by nothing else.

General John Brooks gave up his medical practice to answer the pa-
triot call to fortify Bunker Hill. He also fought with distinction at
White Plains and Saratoga. As a Federalist he served as governor of
the Commonwealth from 1816-1822.

Gen. Brooks, (of Medford), in reply to Gen. Heath, said, he
recollected the passage of Montesquieu, but he also recollected
that that writer had spoken highly of the British government.
He then adverted to the objection of this section of Gen.
Thompson and others, that biennial elections were a novelty,
and said, we were not to consider whether a measure was new,
but whether it was proper. Gentlemen had said that it had been
the established custom of this country to elect annually: but, he

asked, have we not gone from a colonial to an independent situation? We were then provinces, we are now an independent empire; our measures, therefore, says he, must change with our situation. Under our old government, the objects of legislation were few, and divided; under our present, they are many, and must be united; and it appears necessary that, according to the magnitude and multiplicity of the business, the duration should be extended – he did not, he said, undertake to say how far. He then went into a view of the history of Parliaments. The modern northern nations, he said, had parliaments, but they were called by their kings, and the time, business, &c., of them, depended wholly on their wills. We can, therefore, says he, establish nothing from these. One general remark was, that in the reigns of weak princes, the power and importance of parliaments increased; in the reigns of strong and arbitrary kings, they have always declined; and, says he, they have been *triennial*, and they have been *septennial*. The General combated the idea, *that the liberties of the people depended on the duration of parliament*, with much ability. Do we hear, asked he, that the people of England are deprived of their liberties – or that they are not as free now as when they had short parliaments? On the contrary, do not writers agree that life, liberty and property are no where better secured than in Great Britain – and that this security arises from their parliaments being chosen for seven years. As such is the situation of the people of England, and as no instance can be given wherein biennial elections have been destructive to the liberties of the people, he concluded by asking, whether so much danger is to be apprehended from such elections as gentlemen imagined?

Thompson angered the Federalists by using Shays' Rebellion as an example of the need for annual elections.

Sir, gentlemen have said a great deal about the history of old times. I confess, I am not acquainted with such history – but I am, Sir, acquainted with the history of my own country. I had the honor to be in the general court last year, and am in it this year. I think, Sir, that had the last administration continued one year longer, our liberties would have been lost, and the country involved in blood: not so much, Sir, from their bad conduct, but from the suspicions of the people of them. But, Sir, a change took place; from this change pardons have been granted to the people, and peace is restored. This, Sir, I say, is in favor of frequent elections.

Wealthy, conservative Christopher Gore received the least votes of the town of Boston's twelve delegates. Although he was only 29 years old in 1788, Gore already had assumed the posture of a "Great Man," complete with magnificent residences (a townhouse near the Boston Common and a country house in Waltham), liveried servants, splendid carriages, and political speeches studded with classical allusions.

It has been observed, that in considering this great and momentous question, we ought to consult the sentiments of wise men, who have written on the subject of government, and thereby regulate our decision on this business. A passage is adduced from Montesquieu, stating, that where the people delegate great power, it ought to be compensated for by the shortness of the duration. Though strictly agreeing with the author, I do not see that it applies to the subject under consideration. This might be perfectly applicable to the ancient governments, where they had no idea of representation, or different checks in the legislature or administration of government; but in the proposed Constitution, the powers of the whole government are limited to certain national objects, and are accurately defined; the House of Representatives is but one branch of the system, and can do nothing of itself; Montesquieu, in the sentiment alluded to, must have had in his mind the Epistates of Athens, or the Dictators of Rome, but certainly observations drawn from such sources can have no weight in considering things so essentially different. Again, Sir, gentlemen have said, that annual elections were necessary to the preservation of liberty, and that in proportion as the people of different nations have lengthened, beyond the term of a year, the duration of their representatives, they have lost their liberties, and that all writers have agreed in this. I may mistake, but I know no such thing as a representation of the people in any of the ancient republics. In England, from whence we receive many of our ideas on this subject, King John covenanted with his people to summons certain classes of men to parliament. By the constitution of that country, the king alone can convoke, and he alone, previous to the revolution, could dissolve, the parliament; but in the reign of William III, the patriots obtained an act limiting the duration of parliaments to three years. Soon after, a parliament then sitting and near expiring, a rebellion broke out, and the tories and Jacobites were gaining strength to support the Pretender's claim to the crown. Had they dissolved themselves, and a new parliament been convoked, probably many of the very opponents to the government might have been elected. In that case, they might have effected by law, what they in vain attempted by arms.

The parliament, therefore, extended their duration from triennial to septennial; this was acquiesced in by the people, and the next parliament sanctified the act. No evil, but great good, has been supposed to follow from their duration being thus extended; and if Montesquieu and Doctor Adams think the British Constitution so perfect, how much greater must be our security, when we reflect that our representation is equal; that the powers of the government are so limited, and the checks so nicely appointed. If there be a representation of the people in any other countries, and annual elections therein have been considered as the basis of their freedom, I pray gentlemen to mention the instances; I confess I know none. People adopt a position which is certainly true, viz.: that elections ought to be frequent; but then, as we have been in the custom of choosing our representatives annually, we have determined annually to be frequent, and that biennally, or any longer term than annual, is not frequent. But if gentlemen will only consider the objects over which this government is to have rule and authority, and the immense and wide extended tracts of country over which the representatives are to pass before they reach the seat of government, I think they will be convinced that two years is a short time for the representatives to hold their office. Further, Sir, we must consider this subject with respect to the general structure of the Constitution. The Senate represents the sovereignty of the States; the House of Representatives the people of the United States. The former have a longer term in their office; it is then necessary that that body which represents the people should have a permanence in their office to resist any operations of the Senate which might be injurious to the people. If they were annual, I submit it to the good sense of this house, whether they would be able to preserve that weight in the system, which the Constitution intended they should have, and which is absolutely necessary for the security of the rights of the people.

Elections: Who Regulates?
ARTICLE I, SECTION 4

Ebenezer Pierce, an Antifederalist from a small town in Berkshire County, saw Congress' power to regulate elections as another way in which the proposed Constitution would give the national government uncontrollable power.

Mr. Pierce, (from Partridgefield,) after reading the fourth section wished to know the opinion of gentlemen on it; as Congress appeared thereby to have a power to regulate the *time, place* and *manner* of holding elections. In respect to the manner, said Mr. Pierce, suppose the legislature of this State should prescribe that the choice of the Federal Representatives should be in the same manner as that of Governor – a majority of all the votes in the State being necessary to make it such – and Congress should deem it an improper *manner*, and should order that it be as practiced in several of the Southern States, where the highest number of votes makes a choice – have they not power by this section so to do? Again, as to the *place*, continues Mr. Pierce, may not Congress direct that the election for Massachusetts shall be held in Boston? And if so, it is possible that previous to the election, a number of electors may meet, agree upon the eight delegates, and propose the same to a few towns in the vicinity, who, agreeing in sentiment, may meet on the day of election, and carry their list by a major vote. He did not, he said, say that this would be the case; but he wished to know if it was not a possible one. As the Federal Representatives, who are to form the democratical part of the general government, are to be a check on the representatives of the sovereignty, the Senate, he thought the utmost caution ought to be used, to have their elections as free as possible. He observed, that as men have been ever fond of power, we must suppose they ever will continue so; and concluded by observing, that our caution ought in the present case to be greater, as by the proposed Constitution no qualification of property was required in a representative; and it might be in the power of some people thereby to choose a bankrupt for their representative, in order to give such representative employment, or that he might make laws favorable to such a description of people.

Smallpox had impaired the vision of Caleb Strong and poor health had forced him to leave Philadelphia before a draft of the Constitution had been completed, but he was a staunch Federalist who played an important role in Massachusetts.

The power, says he, to regulate the elections of our federal representatives must be lodged somewhere. I know of but two bodies wherein it can be lodged – *the Legislatures of the several States,* and *the General Congress.* If the legislative bodies of the States, who must be supposed to know at what time, and in what place and manner, the elections can best be held, should so appoint them, it cannot be supposed that Congress, by the power granted by this section, will alter them. But if a legislature of a State should refuse to make such regulations, the consequence will be, that the representatives will not be chosen, and the general government will be dissolved. In such case, can gentlemen say that a power to remedy the evil is not necessary to be lodged somewhere? And where can it be lodged but in Congress? I will consider its advantage in another respect: we know, Sir, that a negligence in the appointment of rulers is the characteristic of all nations. In this State, and since the establishment of our present Constitution, the first officers of government have been elected by less than one-tenth part of the electors in the State. We also know that our town meetings, for the choice of officers, are generally attended by an inconsiderable part of the qualified voters. People attend so much to their private interest, that they are apt to neglect this right. Nations have lost their liberties by neglecting their privileges; consequently Congress ought to have an interposing power to awaken the people, when thus negligent. Even supposing, Sir, the provisional clause suggested by the worthy gentleman from Norton, should be added – would not Congress then be the judges whether the elections in the several States were constitutional and proper? If so, it will then stand on the same ground it now does. It appears evident that there must be a general power to regulate general elections. Gentlemen have said, the proposed Constitution was in some places ambiguous. I wish they would point out the particular instances of ambiguity; for my part I think the whole of it is expressed in the plain, common language of mankind. If any parts are not so explicit as they could be, it cannot be attributed to any design; for I believe a great majority of the men who formed it were sincere and honest men.

One of the Antifederalists' most strident critics of the Constitution, William Wedgery was born in England but had served on an American privateer during the Revolution, before he settled in Maine.

Mr. Wedgery insisted that we had a right to be jealous of our rulers, who ought never to have a power which they could abuse. The fourth section ought to have gone further — it ought to have had the provision in it mentioned by Mr. Bishop. [Phaneul Bishop, an Antifederalist from Rehoboth, proposed that Congress be permitted to make laws regulating elections *only* if a state refused or neglected to do so.] There would then be a mutual check: and he still wished it to be further explained. The worthy gentleman contested the similitude made by the honorable gentleman from Newburyport, between the power to be given to Congress by the fourth section, to compel the States to send representatives, and the power given to the legislature by our own Constitution, to oblige towns to send representatives to the general court, by observing that the case was materially different; as, in the latter, if any town refuses to send representatives, a power of fining such town only is given. It is in vain, says Mr. Wedgery, to say that rulers are not subject to passions and prejudices. In the last general court, of which I was a member, I would willingly have deprived the three western counties from sending delegates to this house, as I *then* thought it unnecessary. But, Sir, what would have been the consequence? A large part of the State would have been deprived of their dearest privileges. I mention this, Sir, to show the force of passion and prejudice.

Charles Turner of Scituate began the convention as an Antifederalist, as this speech makes clear. But, although he missed three weeks of the debates because of illness, he switched and voted with the Federalists.

Mr. President: I am pleased with the ingenuity of some gentlemen in defence of this [fourth] section. I am so impressed with the love of liberty so dearly bought, that I heartily acquiesce in compulsory laws, for the people ought to be obliged to attend to their interest. But I do not wish to give Congress a power which they can abuse; and I wish to know whether such a power is not contained in this section. I think it is. I now proceed, Sir, to the consideration of an idea that Congress may alter the place of choosing representatives in the General Congress. They may order that it may be at the extremity of a State, and, by their influence, may there prevail, that persons may be chosen who otherwise would not by reason that a part of the qualified voters in part of the State would be so incommoded thereby, as to be debarred from their right, as much as if they were bound at home. If so, such a circumstance would militate against the Constitution, which allows every man to vote. Altering the place, will put it so far in the power of Congress as that the representatives chosen will not be the true and genuine representatives of the people, but creatures of the Congress; and so far as they are so, so far are the people deprived of their rights, and the choice will be made in an irregular and unconstitutional manner. When this alteration is made by Congress, may we not suppose whose reëlection will be provided for? Would it not be for those who were chosen before? The great law of self-preservation will prevail. It is true, they might, one time in a hundred, provide for a friend, but most commonly for themselves. But, however honorable the Convention may be who proposed this article, I think it is a genuine power for Congress to perpetuate themselves; a power that cannot be unexceptionably exercised in any case whatever. Knowing the numerous arts that designing men are prone to, to secure their election, and perpetuate themselves, it is my hearty wish that a rotation may be provided for. I respect and revere the Convention who proposed this Constitution. In order that the power given to Congress may be more palatable, some gentlemen are pleased to hold up the idea that we may be blessed with sober, solid, upright men in Congress. I wish that we may be favored with such rulers; but I fear they will not all, if most, be the best moral or political characters. It gives me pain, and I believe it gives pain to others, thus to characterize the country in which I was born. I will endeavor to guard against any injurious reflections against my fellow-citizens. But they must have their true characters; and if I represent them wrong, I am willing to make concessions. I think that the operation of paper money, and the practice of privateering, have produced a gradual decay of morals, introduced pride, ambition, envy, lust of power, produced a decay of patriotism and the love of commutative justice; and I am apprehensive these are the invariable concomitants of the luxury in which we are unblessedly involved, almost to our total destruction. In the lower ranks of people, luxury and avarice operate to the want of public duty and the payment of debts. These demonstrate the necessity of an energetic government. As people become more luxurious, they become more incapacitated for governing themselves. And are we not so? Alike people, alike prince. But suppose it should so happen that the administrators of this Constitution should be preferable to the corrupt mass of the people, in point of manners, morals and rectitude; power will give a keen edge to the principles I have mentioned. Ought we not, then, to put all checks and controls on governors, for the public safety? Therefore, instead of giving Congress powers they may not abuse, we ought to withhold our hands from granting such as must be abused if exercised.

Elections: How Many Representatives?
ARTICLE I, SECTION 2

The Rev. Jeremy Belknap characterized Taylor as "cunning and loquacious," although this speech is straightforward and brief. Taylor believed that in order to mirror the wishes of the people, the number of representatives should be more numerous than provided by the Constitution.

Dr. Taylor thought that the number of members to be chosen for the House of Representatives was too small. The whole Union was entitled to send but sixty-five; whereas, by the old Confederation, they send ninety-one; a reduction of thirty per cent. He had heard it objected, that if a larger number were sent, the house would be unwieldy. He thought our House of

Representatives, which sometimes consists of one hundred and fifty, was not unwieldy; and if the number of the Federal representatives was enlarged to twice sixty-five, he thought it would not be too large. He then proceeded to answer another objection, "that an increase of numbers would be an increase of expense," and by calculation demonstrated that the salaries of the full number he wished, would, in a year, amount only to £2,980 — about one penny on a poll; and by this increase, he thought every part of the Commonwealth would be represented. The distresses of the people would thereby be more fully known and relieved.

Francis Dana was an eccentric Federalist. Like other conservative, wealthy judges, he traveled around his circuit in the style of an English lord and lived in a splendid mansion in Cambridge. But Dana also sported a spurious coat of arms and carried a gold-headed cane and a white fur muff.

Judge Dana, remarking on the assertions of Dr. Taylor, that the number of representatives was too small, that the whole Union was now entitled to send but sixty-five, whereas by the Confederation they might send ninety-one, a reduction of thirty per cent., said, if the Constitution under consideration was, in fact, what its opposers had often called it, a consolidation of the States, he should readily agree with that gentleman that the representation of the people was much too small; but this was a charge brought against it without any foundation in truth. So far from it, that it must be apparent to every one, that the Federal government springs out of, and can alone be brought into existence by, the State governments. Demolish the latter, and there is an end of the former. Had the Continental Convention, then, doubled the representation, agreeably to that gentleman's ideas, would not the people of this Commonwealth have been the first to complain of it as an unnecessary burden laid upon them; that, in addition to their own domestic government they had been charged with the support of so numerous a national government. Would they not have contended for the demolition of the one or the other, as being unable to support both. Would they have been satisfied by being told that doubling the representation would yearly amount only "to about one penny upon a poll." Does not the gentleman know that the expense of our own numerous representation has excited much ill will against the government? Has he never heard it said among the people that our public affairs would be as well conducted by half the number of representatives? If he has not, I have, Sir, and believe it to be true. But the gentleman says there is a reduction of thirty per cent. in the Federal representation, as the whole Union can send but sixty-five members, when under the Confederation they may send ninety-one. The gentleman has not made a fair calculation. For if to the sixty-five representatives under the proposed Constitution we add two senators from each State, amounting to twenty-six in all, we shall have the same number, ninety-one, so that in this respect there is no difference. Besides, this representation will increase with the population of the States, and soon become sufficiently large to meet that gentleman's ideas.

The Powers of Congress
ARTICLE I. SECTION 8

Thomas Dawes, Jr. was a lawyer who also sat on the board of directors of the Massachusetts Bank. A delegate from the Federalist stronghold of Boston, he argued that economic prosperity, particularly in Massachusetts, depended upon Congress having ample power to regulate commerce and currency.

Mr. Dawes said, he thought the powers in the paragraph under debate should be fully vested in Congress. We have suffered, said he, for want of such authority in the Federal head. This will be evident if we take a short view of our agriculture, commerce and manufactures. Our agriculture has not been encouraged by the imposition of national duties on rival produce; nor can it be, so long as the several States may make contradictory laws. This has induced our farmers to raise only what they wanted to consume in their own families; I mean, however, after raising enough to pay their taxes; for I insist, that upon the old plan, the land has borne the burden. For, as Congress could not make laws whereby they could obtain a revenue, in their own way, from impost or excise, they multiplied their requisitions on the several States. When a State was thus called on, it would perhaps impose new duties on its own trade, to procure money for paying its quota of Federal demands. This would drive the trade to such neighboring States as made no such new impositions. Thus the revenue would be lost with the trade, and the only resort would be a direct tax.

As to commerce, it is well known that the different States now pursue different systems of duties in regard to each other. By this, and for want of general laws of prohibition through the Union, we have not secured even our own domestic traffic, that passes from State to State. This is contrary to the policy of every nation on earth. Some nations have no other commerce. The great and flourishing empire of China has but little commerce beyond her own territories; and no country is better circumstanced than we, for an exclusive traffic from State to State. Yet even in *this* we are rivalled by foreigners — by those foreigners to whom we are the least indebted. A vessel from Roseway or Halifax finds as hearty a welcome with its fish and whalebone at the southern ports, as though it was built, navigated and freighted from Salem or Boston. And this must be the case, until we have laws comprehending and embracing alike all the States in the Union.

But it is not only our coasting trade; our whole commerce is going to ruin. Congress has not had power to make even a trade-law which shall confine the importation of foreign goods to the ships of the producing or consuming country: if we had such a law, we should not go to England for the goods of other nations; nor would British vessels be the carriers of American produce from our sister States. In the States southward of the Delaware, it is agreed, that three-fourths of the produce are exported, and three-fourths of the returns are made, in British bottoms. It is said, that for exporting timber, one-half of the property goes to the carrier; and of the produce in general, it has been computed, that when it is shipped for London from a southern State, to the value of one million of dollars, the British merchant draws from that sum three hundred thousand dollars, under the names of freight and charges. This is money which belongs to the New England States, because we can furnish the ships as well as, and much better than, the British. Our sister States are willing we should receive these benefits, and that they should be secured to us by national laws; but until that is done, their private merchants will, no doubt, for the sake of long credit, or some other such temporary advantage, prefer the ships of foreigners. And yet we have suffered these ignominious burdens rather than trust our own representatives with power to help us, and we call ourselves free and independent states. We are independent of each other, but we are slaves to Europe. We have no uniformity in duties, imposts, excises or prohibitions. Congress has no authority to withhold advantages from foreigners, in order to obtain advantages from them. By the ninth of the old articles, Congress may enter into treaties and alliances under certain provisos, but Congress cannot pledge that a single State shall not render the whole treaty of commerce a nullity.

Our manufactures are another great subject, which has received no encouragement by national duties on foreign manufactures, and they never can by any authority in the Confederation. It has been said, that no country can produce manufactures until it be overstocked with inhabitants. It is true, the United States have employment, except in the winter, for their citizens, in agriculture – the most respectable employment under heaven; but it is now to be remembered, that since the old Confederation, there is a great emigration of foreign artisans hither, some of whom are left here by the armies of the last war, and others, who have more lately sought the new world, from hopes of mending their condition. These will not change their employments. Besides this, the very face of our country leads to manufactures. Our numerous falls of water, and places for mills, where paper, snuff, gunpowder, iron works, and numerous other articles, are prepared – these will save us immense sums of money, that otherwise would go to Europe. The question is, have these been encouraged? Has Congress been able, by national laws, to prevent the importation of such foreign commodities as are made from such raw materials as we ourselves raise? It is alleged, that the citizens of the United States have contracted debts within the last three years, with the subjects of Great Britain, for the amount of near six millions of dollars, and that consequently our lands are mortgaged for that sum. So Corsica was once mortgaged to the Genoese merchants for articles which her inhabitants did not want, or which they could have made themselves, and she was afterwards sold to a foreign power. If we wish to encourage our own manufactures – to preserve our own commerce – to raise the value of our own lands – we must give Congress the powers in question.

The honorable gentleman from Norton, last speaking, says, that if Congress have the power of laying and collecting taxes, they will use the power of the sword. I hold the reverse to be true. The doctrine of requisitions, or of demands upon a whole State, implies such a power; for surely a whole State, a whole community, can be compelled only by an army; but taxes upon an individual, implies only the use of a collector of taxes. That Congress, however, will not apply to the power of direct taxation, unless in cases of emergency, is plain; because, as thirty thousand inhabitants will elect a representative, eight-tenths of which electors perhaps are yeomen, and holders of farms, it will be their own fault if they are not represented by such men as will never permit the land to be injured by unnecessary taxes.

Like other Federalists, Gore feared disorder among the people more than power in the hands of the government. Although Gore was ambitious, he was not unscrupulous. He refused to take part in rumor-mongering about why Governor Hancock supported the Constitution.

This section, Mr. President, has been the subject of many observations, founded on real or pretended jealousies of the powers herein delegated to the general government; and by comparing the proposed Constitution with things in their nature totally different, the mind may be seduced from a just determination on the subject. Gentlemen have compared the authority of Congress, to levy and collect taxes from the people of America, to a similar power assumed by the Parliament of Great Britain. If we but state the relation which these two bodies bear to America, we shall see that no arguments drawn from one, can be applicable to the other. The House of Commons, in the British Parliament, which is the only popular branch of that assembly, was composed of men chosen exclusively by the inhabitants of Great Britain, in no sort amenable to, or dependent upon, the people of America, and secured, by their local situation, from every burden they might lay on this country. By impositions on this part of the empire, they might be relieved from their own taxes, but could in no case be injured themselves.

The Congress of the United States is to be chosen, either mediately or immediately, by the people. They can impose no burdens but what they participate in, in common with their fellow-citizens. The senators and representatives, during the time for which they shall be elected, are incapable of holding any office which shall be created, or the emolument of which shall be increased, during such time. This is taking from candidates every lure to office, and from the administrators of the government, every temptation to create or increase emoluments to such degree as shall be burdensome to their constituents. Gentlemen, who candidly consider these things, will not say that arguments against the assumption of power by Great Britain can apply to the Congress of the United States.

Some gentlemen suppose it is unsafe and unnecessary to vest the proposed government with authority to "lay and collect taxes, duties, imposts and excises." Let us strip the subject of every thing that is foreign, and refrain from likening it with governments which in their nature and administration have no affinity; and we shall soon see that it is not only safe, but indispensably necessary to our peace and dignity, to vest the Congress with the powers described in this section. To determine the necessity of investing that body with the authority alluded to, let us inquire what duties are incumbent on them. To pay the debts, and provide for the common defence and general welfare of the United States; to declare war, &c.; to raise and support armies; to provide and maintain a navy: these are authorities and duties incident to every government. No one has, or I presume will, deny that whatever government may be established over America ought to perform such duties. The expense attending these duties is not within the power of calculation. The exigencies of government are in their nature illimitable; so then must be the authority which can meet these exigencies. Where we demand an object, we must afford the means necessary to its attainment. Whenever it can be clearly ascertained, what will be the future exigencies of government, the expense attending them, and the product of any particular tax, duty or impost, then, and not before, can the people of America limit their government to amount and fund. Some have said that the impost and excise would be sufficient for all the purposes of government in the times of peace; and that in war, requisitions should be made on the several States for sums to supply the deficiencies of this fund. Those who are best informed, suppose this fund inadequate to, and none pretend that it can exceed, the expenses of a peace establishment. What then is to be done? Is America to wait until she is attacked, before she attempts a preparation for defence? This would certainly be unwise; it would be courting our enemies to make war upon us. The operations of war are sudden, and call for large sums of money. Collections from States are at all times slow and uncertain; and in case of refusal, the non-complying State must be coerced by arms, which in its consequences would involve the innocent with the guilty, and introduce all the horrors of a civil war. But it is said, we need not fear a war — we have no enemies. Let gentlemen consider the situation of our country; they will find we are circumscribed with enemies, from Maine to Georgia. I trust, therefore, that upon a fair and candid consideration of the subject, it will be found indispensibly requisite to the peace, dignity and happiness of America, that the proposed government should be vested with all the powers granted by the section under debate.

Samuel Thompson of Topsham, Maine, was a self-made man who had been commissioned a brigadier general during the Revolution. In the Massachusetts General Court, Thompson had earned a reputation as an obstinate, angry debater.

Sir, the question is, whether Congress shall have power. Some say, that if this section was left out, the whole would fall to the ground. I think so too, as it is all of a piece. We are now fixing a national consolidation. This section, I look upon it, is big with mischiefs. Congress will have power to keep standing armies. The great Mr. Pitt says standing armies are dangerous. Keep your militia in order — we don't want standing armies. A gentleman said, we are a rich State. I say so too. Then why shall we not wait five or six months, and see what our sister States do? We are able to stand our own ground against a foreign power. They cannot starve us out — they cannot bring their ships on the land — we are a nation of healthy, strong men — our land is fertile, and we are increasing in numbers. It is said we owe money; no matter if we do; our safety lies in not paying it. Pay only the interest. Don't let us go too fast. Shall not Massachusetts be a mediator? It is my wish she may be one of the four dissenting States; then we shall be on our old ground, and shall not act unconstitutionally. Some people cry, it will be a great charge; but it will be a greater charge, and be more dangerous to make a new one. Let us amend the old Confederation. Why not give Congress power only to regulate trade? Some say, that those we owe will fall upon us; but it is no such thing; the balance of power in the old countries will not permit it — the other nations will protect us. Besides, we are a brave and a happy people. Let us be cautious how we divide the States. By uniting we stand, by dividing we fall. We are in our childhood yet; don't let us grow too fast, lest we grow out of shape. If I have proved that we are a respectable people, in possession of liberty, property and virtue, and none in a better situation to defend themselves, why all this racket? Gentlemen say we are undone if we cannot stop up the Thames: But, Mr. President, nations will mind their own interest, and not ours. Great Britain has found out the secret to pick the subjects' pockets, without their knowing of it — that's the very thing Congress is after. Gentlemen say this section is as clear as the sun, and that all power is retained which is not given. But where is the bill of rights which shall check the power of this Congress, which shall say, *thus far shall ye come, and no farther?* The safety of the people depends on a bill of rights. If we build on a sandy foundation, is it likely we shall stand? I appeal to the feelings of the Convention. There are some parts of this Constitution which I cannot digest; and, Sir, shall we swallow a large bone for the sake of a little meat? Some say, swallow the whole now, and pick out the bone afterwards. But I say, let us pick off the meat, and throw the bone away.

This section, Sir, takes the purse-strings from the people. England has been quoted for their fidelity; but did their Constitution ever give such a power as is contained in this Constitution? Did they ever allow Parliament to vote an army but for one year? But here we are giving Congress power to vote an army for two years — to tax us without limitation — no one to gainsay them, and no inquiry yearly, as in Britain. Therefore, if this Constitution is got down, we shall alter the system entirely, and have no checks upon Congress.

Amos Singletary disliked lawyers. After all, he and other Shaysites had been dragged into court for debt and squeezed by lawyers eager to please their eastern clients. Now, he and the Antifederalists believed that these smooth-talking, ambitious men were going to control the new government.

Mr. President: I should not have troubled the Convention again, if some gentlemen had not called upon them that were on the stage in the beginning of our troubles, in the year 1775. I was one of them. I have had the honor to be a member of the court all the time, Mr. President, and I say, that if any body had proposed such a Constitution as this, in that day, it would have been thrown away at once. It would not have been looked at. We contended with Great Britain, some said, for a three-penny duty on tea; but it was not that — it was because they claimed a right to tax us and bind us in all cases whatever. And does not this Constitution do the same? Does it not take away all we have, all our property? Does it not lay *all* taxes, duties, imposts and excises? And what more have we to give? They tell us Congress won't lay dry taxes upon us, but collect all the money they want by impost. I say there has always been a difficulty about impost. Whenever the general court was agoing to lay an impost, they would tell us it was more than trade could bear, that it hurt the fair trader, and encouraged smuggling; and there will always be the same objection — they won't be able to raise money enough by impost, and then they will lay it on the land, and take all we have got. These lawyers, and men of learning, and moneyed men, that talk so finely, and gloss over matters so smoothly, to make us, poor illiterate people, swallow down the pill, expect to get into Congress themselves; they expect to be the managers of this Constitution, and get all the power and all the money into their own hands, and then they will swallow up all us little folks, like the great leviathan, Mr. President; yes, just as the whale swallowed up Jonah. This is what I am afraid of; but I won't say any more at present, but reserve the rest to another opportunity.

Jonathan Smith of Lanesborough was one of only a handful of delegates from Berkshire County to vote for the Constitution. His folksy speech must have been appealing to farmers who, like Smith, prided themselves on their independent minds.

Mr. President: I am a plain man and get my living by the plough. I am not used to speak in public, but I beg your leave to say a few words to my brother plough-joggers in this house. I have lived in a part of the country where I have known the worth of good government by the want of it. There was a black cloud that rose in the east last winter, and spread over the west. [Here Mr. Wedgery interrupted: Mr. President, I wish to know what the gentleman means by the east?] I mean, Sir, the county of Bristol. The cloud rose there, and burst upon us, and produced a dreadful effect. It brought on a state of anarchy, and that leads to tyranny. I say, it brought anarchy. People that used to live peaceably, and were before good neighbors, got distracted, and took up arms against government. [Here Mr. Kinsley called to order, and asked, what had the history of last winter to do with the Constitution? Several gentlemen, and among the rest, the Hon. Mr. Adams, said the gentleman was in order, let him go on in his own way.] I am agoing, Mr. President, to show you, my brother farmers, what were the effects of anarchy, that you may see the reasons why I wish for good government. People, I say, took up arms, and then, if you went to speak to them, you had the musket of death presented to your breast. They would rob you of your property, threaten to burn your houses; oblige you to be on your guard night and day; alarms spread from town to town; families were broke up; the tender mother would cry: O, my son is among them! What shall I do for my child! Some were taken captive, children taken out of their schools and carried away. Then we should hear of an action, and the poor prisoners were set in the front, to be killed by their own friends. How dreadful, how distressing was this! Our distress was so great that we should have been glad to snatch at any thing that looked like a government, for protection. Had any person, that was able to protect us, come and set up his standard, we should all have flocked to it, even if it had been a *monarch*, and that monarch might have proved a tyrant; so that you see that anarchy leads to tyranny; it is better to have *one* tyrant than so many at once.

Now, Mr. President, when I saw this Constitution, I found that it was a cure for these disorders. It was just such a thing as we wanted. I got a copy of it and read it over and over. I had been a member of the Convention to form our own State Constitution, and had learnt something of the checks and balances of power, and I found them all here. I did not go to any lawyer, to ask his opinion; we have no lawyer in our town, and we do well enough without. I formed my own opinion, and was pleased with this Constitution. My honorable old daddy there (pointing to Mr. Singletary) won't think that I expect to be a Congressman, and swallow up the liberties of the people. I never had any post, nor do I want one, and before I am done you will think that I don't deserve one. But I don't think the worse of the Constitution because lawyers, and men of learning, and moneyed men, are fond of it. I don't suspect that they want to get into Congress and abuse their power. I am not of such a jealous make. They that are honest men themselves are not apt to suspect other people. I don't know why our constituents have not as good a right to be jealous of us, as we seem to be of the Congress, and I think those gentlemen who are so very suspicious that as soon as a man gets into power he turns rogue, had better look at home.

We are by this Constitution allowed to send ten members to Congress. Have we not more than that number fit to go? I dare say, if we pick out ten, we shall have another ten left, and I hope ten times ten – and will not these be a check upon those that go? Will they go to Congress and abuse their power, and do mischief, when they know that they must return and look the other ten in the face, and be called to account for their conduct? Some gentlemen think that our liberty and property are not safe in the hands of moneyed men, and men of learning. I am not of that mind.

Brother farmers, let us suppose a case now: Suppose you had a farm of fifty acres, and your title was disputed, and there was a farm of five thousand acres joined to you, that belonged to a man of learning, and his title was involved in the same difficulty; would not you be glad to have him for your friend, rather than to stand alone in the dispute? Well, the case is the same; these lawyers, these moneyed men, these men of learning, are all embarked in the same cause with us, and we must all swim or sink together; and shall we throw the Constitution overboard because it does not please us alike? Suppose two or three of you had been at the pains to break up a piece of rough land, and sow it with wheat; would you let it lie waste, because you could not agree what sort of a fence to make? Would it not be better to put up a fence that did not please every one's fancy, rather than not fence it at all, or keep disputing about it, until the wild beasts came in and devoured it. Some gentlemen say — don't be in a hurry, take time to consider, and don't take a leap in the dark. I say — take things in time, gather fruit when it is ripe. There is a time to sow, and a time to reap. We sowed our seed when we sent men to the Federal Convention; now is the harvest, now is the time to reap the fruit of our labor, and if we don't do it now, I am afraid we never shall have another opportunity.

The Existence of Slavery
ARTICLE I, SECTION 9

James Neal, a Maine Quaker, told the convention that "how much soever he liked the other parts of the Constitution," he would vote against ratification unless the clause extending the slave trade for 20 years was removed. He kept his word.

His profession, he said, obliged him to bear witness against any thing that should favor the making merchandise of the bodies of men; and unless his objection was removed, he could not put his hand to the Constitution. Other gentlemen said, in addition to this idea, that there was not even a provision that the negroes ever shall be free; and Samuel Thompson echoed the anti-slavery sentiments of his colleague.

Gen. Thompson exclaimed — Mr. President: Shall it be said, that after we have established our own independence and freedom, we make slaves of others? O, Washington, what a name has he had! How he has immortalized himself! But he holds those in slavery who have as good right to be free as he has. He is still for self, and, in my opinion, his character has sunk fifty per cent.

General William Heath of Roxbury articulated the Federalist position on slavery; it was an abominable evil, but unless it was protected where it existed, the southern states would not join the union.

Mr. President: The paragraph respecting the migration or importation of such persons as any of the States now existing shall think proper to admit, &c., is one of those considered during my absence, and I have heard nothing on the subject, save what has been mentioned this morning; but I think the gentlemen who have spoken, have carried the matter rather too far on both sides. I apprehend that it is not in our power to do any thing for or against those who are in slavery in the southern States. No gentleman within these walls detests every idea of slavery more than I do; it is generally detested by the people of this Commonwealth; and I ardently hope that the time will soon come, when our brethren in the southern States will view it as we do, and put a stop to it; but to this we have no right to compel them. Two questions naturally arise, if we ratify the Constitution: Shall we do any thing by our act to hold the blacks in slavery? or shall we become partakers of other men's sins? I think neither of them. Each State is sovereign and independent to a certain degree, and they have a right, and will regulate their own internal affairs, as to themselves appears proper; and shall we refuse to eat, or to drink, or to be united, with those who do not think or act just as we do? Surely not. We are not in this case partakers of other men's sins, for in nothing do we voluntarily encourage the slavery of our fellow men. A restriction is laid on the Federal government, which could not be avoided, and a union take place. The Federal Convention went as far as they could. The migration or importation, &c., is confined to the States *now existing* only; new States cannot claim it. Congress, by their ordinance for erecting new States, some time since declared that the new States shall be republican, and that there shall be no slavery in them. But whether those in slavery in the southern States will be emancipated after the year 1808, I do not pretend to determine. I rather doubt it.

The Nature of the Judiciary
ARTICLE III

Abraham Holmes, an Antifederalist delegate from Rochester, Plymouth County, attacked the proposed federal judicial system. Not only did Holmes believe that Article III was riddled with loopholes, he also argued that it made possible arbitrary assaults on individual citizens.

Mr. President: I rise to make some remarks on the paragraph

under consideration, which treats of the judicary power.

It is a maxim universally admitted, that the safety of the subject consists in having a right to a trial as free and impartial as the lot of humanity will admit of. Does the Constitution make provision for such a trial? I think not: for in a criminal process a person shall not have a right to insist on a trial in the vicinity where the fact was committed, where a jury of the peers would, from their local situation, have an opportunity to form a judgment of the character of the person charged with the crime, and also to judge of the credibility of the witnesses. There a person must be tried by a jury of strangers — a jury who may be interested in his conviction; and where he may, by reason of the distance of his residence from the place of trial, be incapable of making such a defence as he is in justice entitled to, and which he could avail himself of, if his trial was in the same county where the crime is said to have been committed.

These circumstances, as horrid as they are, are rendered still more dark and gloomy, as there is no provision made in the Constitution to prevent the attorney-general from filing information against any person, whether he is indicted by the grand jury or not; in consequence of which the most innocent person in the Commonwealth may be taken by virtue of a warrant issued in consequence of such information, and dragged from his home, his friends, his acquaintance, and confined in prison, until the next session of the court which has jurisdiction of the crime with which he is charged, (and how frequent those sessions are to be, we are not yet informed of,) and after long, tedious and painful imprisonment, though acquitted on trial, may have no possibility to obtain any kind of satisfaction for the loss of his liberty, the loss of his time, great expenses, and perhaps cruel sufferings.

But what makes the matter still more alarming is that the mode of criminal process is to be pointed out by Congress, and they have no constitutional check on them, except that the trial is to be a jury; but who this jury is to be, how qualified, where to live, how appointed, or by what rules to regulate their procedure, we are ignorant of as yet; whether they are to be chosen by certain districts; or whether they are to be appointed by the sheriff *ex officio;* whether they are to be for one session of the court only, or for a certain term of time, or for good behavior, or during pleasure; are matters which we are entirely ignorant of as yet.

The mode of trial is altogether indetermined. Whether the criminal is to be allowed the benefit of counsel; whether he is to be allowed to meet his accuser face to face; whether he is to be allowed to confront the witnesses, and have the advantage of cross-examination, we are not yet told.

These are matters by no means of small consequence, yet we have not the smallest constitutional security that we shall be allowed the exercise of these privileges, neither is it made certain in the Constitution, that a person, charged with a crime, shall have the privilege of appearing before the court or jury which is to try him.

On the whole, when we fully consider this matter, and fully investigate the powers granted, explicitly given, and specially delegated, we shall find Congress possessed of powers enabling them to institute judicatories, little less inauspicious than a certain tribunal in Spain, which has long been the disgrace of Christendom: I mean that diabolical institution, the *Inquisition.*

Mr. Gore observed, in reply to Mr. Holmes, that it had been the uniform conduct of those in opposition to the proposed form of government, to determine, in every case where it was possible that the administrators thereof could do wrong, that they would do so, although it were demonstrable that such wrong would be against their own honor and interest, and productive of no advantage to themselves. On this principle alone have they determined that the trial by jury would be taken away in civil cases, when it had been clearly shown that no words could be adopted, apt to the situation and customs of each State in this particular. Jurors are differently chosen in different States, and in point of qualification the laws of the several States are very diverse; not less so, in the causes and disputes which are entitled to trial by jury. What is the result of this? That the laws of Congress may and will be conformable to the local laws in this particular, although the Constitution could not make an universal rule equally applying to the customs and statutes of the different States. Very few governments (certainly not this) can be interested in depriving the people of trial by jury in questions of *meum et tuum.* In criminal cases alone are they interested to have trial under their own control; and in such cases the Constitution expressly stipulates for trial by jury. But then, says the gentleman from Rochester, (Mr. Holmes,) to the safety of life it is indispensably necessary the trial of crimes should be in the vicinity — and the vicinity is construed to mean county. This is very incorrect, and gentlemen will see the impropriety, by referring themselves to the different local divisions and districts of the several States. But further, said the gentleman, the idea that the jury, coming from the neighborhood, and knowing the character and circumstances of the party in trial, is promotive of justice, on reflection will appear not founded in truth. If the jury judge from any other circumstances but what are part of the cause in question, they are not impartial. The great object is, to determine on the real merits of the cause, uninfluenced by any personal considerations. If, therefore, the jury could be perfectly ignorant of the person in trial, a just decision would be more probable. From such motives did the wise Athenians so constitute the famed Areopagus, that when in judgment, this court should sit at midnight, and in total darkness, that the decision might be on the thing, and not on the person. Further, said the gentleman, it has been said, because the Constitution does not expressly provide for an indictment by grand jury in criminal cases, therefore some officer under this government will be authorized to file informations and bring any man to jeopardy of his life, and indictment by grand jury will be disused. If gentlemen who pretend such fears, will look into the Constitution of Massachusetts, they will see that no provision is therein made for an indictment by grand jury, or to oppose the danger of an attorney-general filing informations; yet no difficulty or danger has arisen to the people of this Commonwealth from this defect, if gentlemen please to call it so. If gentlemen would be candid, and not consider that wherever Congress may possibly abuse power, that they certainly will, there would be no difficulty in the minds of any in adopting the proposed Constitution.

Dawes, who was later appointed a Justice of the Supreme Judicial Court, defended the creation of a national judicial system.

Mr. Dawes said, he did not see that the right of trial by jury was taken away by the article. The word *court* does not, either by a popular or technical construction, exclude the use of a jury to try facts. When people in common language talk of a trial at the court of common pleas, or the supreme judicial court, do they not include all the branches and members of such court, the jurors, as well as the judges? They certainly do, whether they mention the jurors expressly or not. Our State legislature have construed the word court in the same way; for they have given appeals from a justice of peace to the court of common pleas, and from thence to the supreme court, without saying any thing of the jury. But in cases which, almost time out of mind, have been tried without jury, there the jurisdiction is given expressly to the justices of a particular court, as may be instanced by suits upon the absconding act, so called.

Gentlemen have compared the article under consideration to that power which the British claimed, and which we resisted at the Revolution, namely, the power of trying the Americans without a jury. But surely there is no parallel in the cases; it was *criminal* cases in which they attempted to make this abuse of power. Mr. Dawes mentioned one example of this, which, though young, he well remembered, and that was the case of Nickerson, the pirate, who was tried without a jury, and whose judges were the governors of Massachusetts, and of some neighboring provinces, together with Admiral Montague, and some gentlemen of distinction. Although this trial was without a jury, yet, as it was a trial upon the civil law, there was not so much clamor about it, as otherwise there might have been; but still it was disagreeable to the people, and was one ground of the then complaints. But the trial by jury was not attempted to be taken from *civil* causes. It was no object of power, whether one subject's property was lessened, while another's was increased; nor can it now be an object with the Federal legislature. What interest can they have in constituting a judiciary, to proceed in civil cases without a trial by jury? In criminal causes by the proposed government, there must be a jury. It is asked, why is not the Constitution as explicit in securing the right of jury in civil, as in criminal cases? The answer is: Because it was out of the power of the Convention. The several States differ so widely in their modes of trial, some States using a jury in causes wherein other States employ only their judges, that the Convention have very wisely left it to the Federal legislature to make such regulations as shall, as far as possible, accommodate the whole. Thus our own State Constitution authorizes the general court to erect judicatories, but leaves the nature, the number and extent of them wholly to the discretion the legislature. The bill of rights indeed secures the trial by jury in civil causes, except in cases where a contrary practice has obtained. Such a clause as this some gentlemen wish were inserted in the proposed Constitution; but such a clause would be absurd in that Constitution as has been clearly stated by the honorable gentleman from Charlestown, (Mr. Gorham,) because the "exception of all cases where a jury have not heretofore been used," would include almost all cases that could be mentioned, when applied to all States, for they have severally differed in the kinds of causes where they have tried without jury.

Hancock's Amendments

He was Boston's favorite son. Frail and in poor health, John Hancock stayed away from the debates over the Constitution until January 31 when he assumed the chair as President of the Convention. He was carried bodily into the hall, "wrapped in his flannels." Although his friends may have alluded to the possibility of high national office, it was Hancock's patriotism and the specter of what might happen to the new nation if the Constitution were rejected that brought him to the convention with a series of amendments designed to "remove the fears and quiet the apprehensions" of the people.

The Convention having impartially discussed and fully considered the Constitution for the United States of America, reported to Congress by the Convention of Delegates from the United States of America, and submitted to us by a Resolution of the General Court of the said Commonwealth, passed the twenty-fifth day of October last past; and acknowledging, with grateful hearts, the goodness of the Supreme Ruler of the Universe, in affording the people of the United States, in the course of his providence, an opportunity, deliberately and peaceably, without fraud or surprise, of entering into an explicit and solemn compact with each other, by assenting to and ratifying a new constitution, in order to form a more perfect union, establish justice, insure domestic tranquillity, provide for the common defence, promote the general welfare, and secure the blessings of liberty to themselves and their posterity; do, in the name, and in behalf of the people of the Commonwealth of Massachusetts, *assent to* and *ratify* the said CONSTITUTION FOR THE UNITED STATES OF AMERICA.

And as it is the opinion of this Convention that certain amendments and alterations in the said Constitution would remove the fears and quiet the apprehensions of many of the good people of this Commonwealth, and more effectually guard against an undue administration of the federal government; the Convention do therefore recommend that the following alterations and provisions be introduced into the said Constitution: —

First. That it be explicitly declared that all powers not expressly delegated to Congress, are reserved to the several States, to be by them exercised.

Secondly. That there shall be one representative to every thirty thousand persons, until the whole number of representatives amount to ____.

Thirdly. That Congress do not exercise the powers vested in them by the fourth section of the first article, but in cases where a State shall neglect or refuse to make adequate provision for an equal representation of the people, agreeably to this Constitution.

Fourthly. That Congress do not lay direct taxes, but when the moneys arising from the impost and excise are insufficient for the public exigencies.

Fifthly. That Congress erect no company of merchants with exclusive advantages of commerce.

Sixthly. That no person shall be tried for any crime, by which he may incur an infamous punishment, or loss of life, until he be first indicted by a grand jury, except in such cases as may arise in the government and regulation of the land and naval forces.

Seventhly. The Supreme Judicial Federal Court shall have no jurisdiction of causes between citizens of different States, unless the matter in dispute be of the value of ____ dollars, at the least.

Eighthly. In civil actions between citizens of different States, every issue of fact arising in actions at common law, shall be tried by a jury, if the parties, or either of them, request it.

Ninthly. That the words, "without the consent of the Congress," in the last paragraph of the ninth section of the first article, be stricken out.

And the Convention do, in the name and in behalf of the people of this Commonwealth, enjoin it upon their Representatives in Congress, at all times, until the alterations and provisions aforesaid have been considered, agreeably to the fifth article of the said Constitution, to exert all their influence, and use all reasonable and legal methods to obtain a ratification of the said alterations and provisions, in such manner as is provided in the said article.

Sam Adams, the old revolutionary, was the first to speak in favor of Hancock's amendments. Everyone knew he had serious reservations about the proposed Constitution, yet he had said little. The sudden, unexpected death of his son shortly after the convention began understandably must have weighed more heavily on his mind than politics. Now, in the closing hours of the convention, he put aside his personal grief and his own political preferences to speak for his country.

Mr. President: I feel myself happy in contemplating the idea that many benefits will result from your Excellency's conciliatory proposition, to this Commonwealth and to the United States; and I think it ought to precede the motion made by the gentleman from Newburyport, and to be at this time considered by the Convention. I have said, that I have had my doubts of this Constitution. I could not digest every part of it, as readily as some gentlemen; but this, Sir, is my misfortune, not my fault. Other gentlemen have had their doubts, but in my opinion, the proposition submitted, will have a tendency to remove such doubts and to conciliate the minds of the Convention and the people without doors. This subject, Sir, is of the greatest magnitude, and has employed the attention of every rational man in the United States; but the minds of the people are not so well agreed on it as all of us could wish. A proposal of this sort, coming from Massachusetts, from her importance, will have its weight. Four or five States have considered and ratified the Constitution as it stands; but we know there is a diversity of opinion, even in these States, and one of them is greatly agitated. If this Convention should particularize the amendments necessary to be proposed, it appears to me it must have weight in other States where Conventions have not yet met. I have observed the sentiments of gentlemen on the subject as far as Virginia; and I have found that the objections were similar, in the newspapers, and in some of the Conventions. Considering these circumstances, it appears to me that such a measure will have the most salutary effect throughout the Union. It is of the greatest importance that America should still be united in sentiment. I think I have not been heretofore unmindful of the advantage of such an Union. It is essential that the people should be united in the Federal government, to withstand the common enemy, and to preserve their valuable rights and liberties. We find, in the great State of Pennsylvania, one-third of the Convention are opposed to it; should there then be large minorities in the several States, I should fear the consequences of such disunion.

Sir, there are many parts of it I esteem as highly valuable, particularly the article which empowers Congress to regulate commerce, to form treaties, &c. For want of this power in our national head, our friends are grieved and our enemies insult us. Our ambassador at the court of London is considered as a mere cipher, instead of the representative of the United States. Therefore it appears to me, that a power to remedy this evil should be given to Congress, and the remedy applied as soon as possible.

The only difficulty on gentlemen's minds is, whether it is best to accept this Constitution on conditional amendments, or to rely on amendments in future, as the Constitution provides. When I look over the article which provides for a revision, I have my doubts. Suppose, Sir, nine States accept the Constitution without any conditions at all; and the four States should wish to have amendments, where will you find nine States to propose, and the legislatures of nine States to agree to the introduction of amendments? Therefore it seems to me that the expectation of amendments taking place at some future time will be frustrated. [Gov. Hancock's] method, if we take it, will be the most likely to bring about the amendments, as the Conventions of New Hampshire, Rhode Island, New York, Maryland, Virginia and South Carolina, have not yet met. I apprehend, Sir, that these States will be influenced by the proposition which your Excellency has submitted, as the resolutions of Massachusetts have ever had their influence. If this should be the case, the necessary amendments would be introduced more early, and more safely. From these considerations, as your Excellency did not think it proper to make a motion, with submission, I move that the paper read by your Excellency, be now taken under consideration by the Convention.

Hancock and Adams had caused a change in the mood of the convention. For the first time the Federalists had gained the offensive. The Antifederalists Taylor and Wedgery charged that there was no guarantee the amendments would be enacted, and they moved for adjournment, a motion that easily was defeated.

Dr. Taylor liked the idea of amendments; but, he said, he did not see any constitutional door open for the introduction of them by the Convention. He read the several authorities which provided for the meeting of Conventions; but he did not see in any of them, any power given to propose amendments. We are, he said, therefore, treading on unsafe ground to propose them. We must take the whole or reject the whole. The honorable gentleman was in favor of the adjournment; and in a speech of some length, deprecated the consequences, which, he said, must arise if the Constitution was adopted or rejected by a small majority; and that the expenses which would accrue from the adjournment would not exceed 4d. per poll throughout the Commonwealth.

Mr. Wedgery said, he did not see the probability that these amendments would be made, if we had authority to propose them. He considered, he said, that the Convention did not meet for the purpose of recommending amendments, but to adopt or reject the Constitution. He concluded by asking, whether it was probable that those States who had already adopted the Constitution, would be likely to submit amendments?

A Boston delegate, Dr. Charles Jarvis, was influenced by the resolutions of support for the Constitution passed by a mass meeting of Boston's mechanics and tradesmen.

It has been insinuated, Sir, that these amendments have been artfully introduced to lead to a decision which would not otherwise be had. Without stopping to remark on the total want of candor in which such an idea has arisen, let us inquire whether there is even the appearance of reason to support this insinuation. The propositions are annexed, it is true, to the ratification; but the assent is complete and absolute without them. It is not possible it can be otherwise understood by a single member in this honorable body. Gentlemen, therefore, when they make such an unjust observation, do no honor to the sagacity of others. Supposing it possible that any single member can be deceived by such a shallow artifice, permit me to do justice to the purity of intention in which they have arisen, by observing, that I am satisfied nothing can be farther from your Excellency's intentions. The propositions are general, and not local; they are not calculated for the peculiar interests of this State, but with indiscriminate justice comprehend the circumstances of the individual on the banks of the Savannah, as well as of the hardy and industrious husbandman on the margin of the Kennebec. Why then they should not be adopted, I confess I cannot conceive. There is one of them in a particular manner which is very agreeable to me. When we talk of our wanting a bill of rights to the new Constitution, the first article proposed must remove every doubt on this head; as, by positively securing what is not expressly delegated, it leaves nothing to the uncertainty of conjecture, or to the refinements of implication, but is an explicit reservation of every right and privilege which are nearest and most agreeable to the people. There has been scarcely an instance where the influence of Massachusetts has not been felt and acknowledged in the Union. In such a case, her voice will be heard, Sir; and I am fully in sentiment, if these amendments are not engrafted on the Constitution, it will be our own fault. The remaining seven States will have our example before them, and there is a high probability that they, or at least some of them, will take our conduct as a precedent, and will perhaps assume the same mode of procedure. Should this be the fact, their influence will be united to ours. But your delegates will besides be subject to a perpetual instruction, until its object is completed; and it will be always in the power of the people and legislature to renew those instructions. But if they should fail, we must then acquiesce in the decision of the majority; and this is the known condition on which all free governments depend.

Would gentlemen who are opposed to the Constitution wish to have no amendments? This does not agree with their reiterated objections to the proposed system. Or are they afraid, Sir, that these propositions will secure a larger majority? On such an occasion we cannot be too generally united. The Constitution is a great political experiment. The amendments have a tendency to remove many objections which have been made to it; and I hope, Sir, when it is adopted, that they will be annexed to the ratification in the manner which your Excellency has proposed.

Turner, now a Federalist, spoke about his personal conversion.

Mr. President: Being advanced in life, and having endeavored, I hope, with a faithful attention, according to my ability, to assist my country in her trying difficulties and dangers, for more than twenty years; and as for three weeks past my state of health has been such as to render me unable to speak in this assembly, I trust I shall be heard with some indulgence while I express a few sentiments at this solemn crisis. I have been averse to the reception of this Constitution while it was considered merely in its original form; but since the honorable Convention have been pleased to agree to the recommendation of certain amendments, I acknowledge my mind is reconciled. But even thus amended, I still see, or think I see, several imperfections in it, and some which give me pain. Indeed, I never expect to see a Constitution free from imperfections; and, considering the great diversity of local interests, views and habits — considering the unparalleled variety of sentiments among the citizens of the United States — I despair of obtaining a more perfect Constitution than this, at present. And a Constitution preferable to the Confederation must be obtained, and obtained soon, or we shall be an undone people. In my judgment there is a rational probability, a moral certainty, that the proposed amendments will meet the approbation of the several States in the Union. If there is any respect due to the hoary head of Massachusetts, it will undoubtedly have its proper influence in this case. The minds of gentlemen, throughout the nation, must be impressed with such a sense of necessity of all important union, especially in our present circumstances, as must strongly operate in favor of a concurrence. The proposed amendments are of such a liberal, such a generous, such a catholic nature and complexion, they are so congenial to the soul of every man who is possessed of a patriotic regard to the preservation of the just rights and immunities of his country, as well as to the institution of a good and necessary government, that I think they must, they will be universally accepted. When, in connection with this confidence, I consider the deplorable state of our navigation and commerce, and various branches of business thereon dependent, the inglorious and provoking figure we make in the eyes of our European creditors, the degree in which the landed interest is burdened and depreciated, the tendency of depreciating paper and tender acts to destroy mutual confidence, faith and credit, to prevent the circulation of specie, and to overspread the land with an inundation, a chaos of multiform injustice, oppression and knavery; when I consider that want of efficiency there is in our government, as to obliging people seasonably to pay their dues to the public, instead of spending their money in support of luxury and extravagance, of consequence the inability of government to satisfy the just demands of its creditors, and to do it in season, so as to prevent their suffering amazingly by depreciation; in connection with my anxious desires that my ears may be no longer perstringed, nor my heart pained with the cries of the injured, suffering widow and orphan; when I also consider that state of our finances which daily exposes us to become a prey to the despotic humor even of an impotent invader, I find myself constrained to say, before this Assembly, and before God, that I think it my duty to give my vote in favor of this Constitution, with the proposed amendments; and unless some further light shall be thrown in my way to influence my opinion, I shall conduct accordingly.

On February 6, 1788 the debates ended. Hancock's final remarks were eloquent and statesmanlike. The convention ratified the Constitution by a vote of 187 to 168.

Gentlemen — Being now called upon to bring the subject under debate to a decision, by bringing forward the question, I beg your indulgence to close the business with a few words. I am happy that my health has been so far restored, that I am rendered able to meet my fellow-citizens as represented in this Convention. I should have considered it as one of the most distressing misfortunes of my life, to be deprived of giving my aid and support to a system, which, if amended (as I feel assured it will be) according to your proposals, cannot fail to give the people of the United States a greater degree of political freedom, and eventually as much national dignity, as falls to the lot of any nation on the earth. I have not, since I had the honor to be in this place, said much on the important subject before us; all the ideas appertaining to the system, as well those which are against as for it, have been debated upon with so much learning and ability, that the subject is quite exhausted.

But you will permit me, gentlemen, to close the whole with one or two general observations. This I request, not expecting to throw any new light upon the subject, but because it may possibly prevent uneasiness and discordance from taking place amongst us and amongst our constituents.

That a general system of government is indispensably necessary to save our country from ruin, is agreed upon all sides. That the one now to be decided upon has its defects, all agree; but when we consider the variety of interests, and the different habits of the men it is intended for, it would be very singular to have an entire union of sentiment respecting it. Were the people of the United States to delegate the powers proposed to be given, to men who were not dependent on them frequently for elections – to men whose interests, either from rank or title, would differ from that of their fellow-citizens in common – the task of delegating authority would be vastly more difficult; but as the matter now stands, the powers reserved by the people render them secure, and until they themselves become corrupt, they will always have upright and able rulers. I give my assent to the Constitution, in full confidence that the amendments proposed will soon become a part of the system. These amendments being in no wise local, but calculated to give security and ease alike to all the States, I think that all will agree to them.

Suffer me to add, that let the question be decided as it may, there can be no triumph on the one side, or chagrin on the other. Should there be a great division, every good man, every one who loves his country, will be so far from exhibiting extraordinary marks of joy, that he will sincerely lament the want of unanimity, and strenuously endeavor to cultivate a spirit of conciliation, both in Convention, and at home. The people of this Commonwealth are a people of great light, of great intelligence in public business. They know that we have none of us an interest separate from theirs; that it must be our happiness to conduce to theirs; and that we must all rise or fall together. They will never, therefore, forsake the first principle of society, that of being governed by the voice of the majority; and should it be that the proposed form of government should be rejected, they will zealously attempt another. Should it, by the vote now to be taken, be ratified, they will quietly acquiesce, and where they see a want of perfection in it, endeavor in a constitutional way to have it amended.

The question now before you is such as no nation on earth, without the limits of America, has ever had the privilege of deciding upon. As the Supreme Ruler of the Universe has seen fit to bestow upon us this glorious opportunity, let us decide upon it, appealing to him for the rectitude of our intentions, and in humble confidence that he will yet continue to bless and save our country.

Hancock's speech to the General Court later in February, 1788, is filled with a sense of historic purpose and excitement. He now spoke for all the citizens of Massachusetts who rejoiced in the formation of a new nation.

In the beginning of your last session I laid before you the Constitution and frame of government for the United States of America, agreed upon by the late general Convention, and transmitted to me by Congress. As the system was to be submitted to the people, and to be decided upon by their delegates in Convention, I forbore to make any remarks upon it. The Convention which you appointed to deliberate upon that important subject, have concluded their session, after having adopted and ratified the proposed plan, according to their resolution, a copy whereof I have directed the secretary to lay before you.

The obvious imbecility of the Confederation of the United States, has too long given pain to our friends, and pleasure to our enemies; but the forming a new system of government, for so numerous a people, of very different views and habits, spread upon such a vast extent of territory, containing such a great variety of soils, and under such extremes of climate, was a task which nothing less than the dreadful apprehension of losing our national existence, could have compelled the people to undertake.

We can be known to the world only under the appellation of the United States; if we are robbed of the idea of our union, we immediately become separate nations, independent of each other, and no less liable to the depredations of foreign powers, than to wars and bloody contentions amongst ourselves. To pretend to exist as a nation without possessing those powers of coerce which are necessarily incident to the national character, would prove a fatal solecism in politics. The objects of the proposed Constitution are, defence against external enemies, and the promotion of tranquillity and happiness amongst the States. Whether it is well calculated for those important purposes, has been the subject of extensive and learned discussion in the Convention which you appointed. I believe there was never a body of men assembled, with greater purity of intention, or with higher zeal for the public interest. And although when the momentous question was decided, there was a greater division than some expected, yet there appeared a candor, and a spirit of conciliation in the minority, which did them great honor, and afforded a happy presage of unanimity amongst the people at large. Though so many of the members of the late Convention could not feel themselves convinced that they ought to vote for the ratification of this system, yet their opposition was conducted with a candid and manly firmness, and with such marks of integrity and real regard to the public interest, as did them the highest honor, and leaves no reason to suppose that the peace and good order of the government is not their object.

The amendments proposed by the Convention are intended to obtain a constitutional security of the principles to which they refer themselves, and must meet the wishes of all the States. I feel myself assured that they will very early become a part of the Constitution, and when they shall be added to the proposed plan, I shall consider it the most perfect system of government, as to the objects it embraces, that has been known amongst mankind.

Gentlemen:

As that Being in whose hands is the government of all the nations of the earth, and who putteth down one, and raiseth up another, according to His sovereign pleasure, has given to the people of these States a rich and an extensive country; has in a marvellous manner given them a name and a standing among the nations of the world, has blessed them with external peace and internal tranquillity; I hope and pray that the gratitude of their hearts may be expressed by a proper use of those inestimable blessings, by the greatest exertions of patriotism, by forming and supporting institutions for cultivating the human understanding, and for the greatest progress of the arts and sciences, by establishing laws for the support of piety, religion and morality, as well as for punishing vice and wickedness, and by exhibiting on the great theatre of the world, those social, public and private virtues, which give more dignity to a people possessing their own sovereignty, than crowns and diadems afford to sovereign princes.

PART IV

The Bay State and the Union

THE announcement that the convention had voted in favor of ratifying the new Constitution of the United States almost immediately produced a wave of jubilation and good fellowship throughout the town of Boston. This was first obvious among the convention delegates themselves who accepted an invitation to join a number of prominent citizens at a gala reception prepared for them in the Senate Chamber of the nearby State House. During the ensuing festivities any bitterness that might have remained from the often strenuous debates over the pros and cons of ratification quickly gave way to a general spirit of "joy, union, and urbanity." Everyone joined in giving toasts to the happy occasion, and appeared to do so with sincerity and good will. "All appeared willing to bury the hatchet of animosity," wrote the correspondent for the *Massachusetts Centinel*, "and to smoke the calumet of union and love."

Popular Reaction

The reaction of the general public to the news of ratification was even more enthusiastic and unrestrained. As soon as the word was officially proclaimed, the bells in public buildings and churches pealed out the good news for several hours and for the next two days, Friday and Saturday, the town of Boston resounded to the noise of booming cannon and other "demonstrations of joy." Obviously convinced that the new Constitution was truly a "people's" document, members of the general public – average people, working people – banded together in a genuine and spontaneous effort to show their wholehearted approval of the ratification vote. On Thursday, February 7, the very same day the news was announced, the local Committee of Tradesmen met and agreed to circulate notices calling upon mechanics, craftsmen, farmers, and artisans "of every description"

The original Faneuil Hall, completed in 1742, was the gathering place for the townspeople of Boston to celebrate the ratification of the Federal Constitution.

from Boston, as well as from all the adjacent towns, to gather in front of Faneuil Hall the next day at 9 o'clock in the morning. They would then prepare to march through town "in Grand Procession" to demonstrate their approbation of the ratification of the Federal Constitution.

The Grand Procession

Although it was very short notice, a surprisingly large number of farmers, laborers, craftsmen, tradesmen, and mechanics showed up at 9 o'clock the next morning in front of Faneuil Hall. After being formed into a line of march according to their various trades and crafts, they stepped off at 11 o'clock and began their triumphal procession through the winding streets of Boston. There were bands of foresters with their axes, followed by yokes of oxen and clusters of horse-drawn harrows. Sowers, mowers, and winnowers marched along carrying hoes, spades, and scythes, while blacksmiths, shipwrights, rope-makers, sail-makers, painters, carvers, and riggers testified to the maritime character of the town they represented. Mid-way in the procession came a large float of the good ship "Federal Constitution" with full colors flying, drawn along on runners by thirteen horses and followed by the captains of vessels, 85 sailors, and some 250 principal merchants of the town. Behind this assemblage marched about 20 ship-builders with another float drawn by thirteen horses. This represented the old ship of state, "Old Confederation," which was symbolically hauled up for repairs and attended by workmen at various points along its hull. After these floats, the long procession of tradesmen continued as far as the eye could see. There were carpenters and masons, printers and bookbinders, goldsmiths and jewelers, chair-makers and saddlers, leather-dressers and card-makers. Finally, the end of

Boston was not the only town that celebrated its ratification of the Constitution with a replica of the good ship "Constitution." This illustration shows a similar float in a New York parade, drawn along by a team of horses during a tumultuous reception for Alexander Hamilton and the other Federalist supporters of the new Constitution of the United States.

the procession came into view, brought up by the Committee of Tradesmen which had organized the parade, a military band, and a colorful militia unit called the "Republican Volunteers."

The Voice of the People

It was a gala parade that stopped every now and then in front of the house of some distinguished citizen of the town who had represented Boston at the recent ratifying convention, gave "three huzzas," and then fired a salute from the cannon of the ships they were pulling along. As the marchers reached the State House about 2 o'clock, they were greeted by Captain Johnson's company of artillery which was drawn up in formation and fired a 13-gun salute in their honor. According to the *Massachusetts Centinel*, it was about at this point when the people marching in the Grand Procession halted and proclaimed that "Long Lane," the site of the meeting house where the ratifying convention had held its sessions, was henceforth to be called "Federal Street." Starting out with the words *"WE, THE PEOPLE IN GRAND PROCESSION . . . ,"* the announcement was read aloud by the chairman of the Committee of Tradesmen, and was immediately accepted by the townspeople as having the force of law. About 4 o'clock, having been marching steadily for nearly five hours, the procession arrived back at its starting point before Faneuil Hall where refreshments had been "liberally provided." Although the hall was supposed to be able to hold 1500 people, no more than 500 were able to squeeze in to enjoy those refreshments. Those who could not get in, therefore, had to be satisfied with whatever their friends were able to bring out to them.

The End of the "Old Confederation"

Later that evening, the vessel "Old Confederation" that had been exhibited in the procession earlier in the day was hauled up to Boston Common. The officers of the ship, together with the owners and the crew, called upon a jury of carpenters to inspect the vessel and give a report of her condition. After inspecting the ship from top to bottom, the jury announced to the assembled throng that her bottom was so defective and her timbers so completely rotted that the "Old Confederation" – like the former government she symbolized – was "unfit for any further service." The old ship was thereupon summarily ordered to be burned, and to the delight of the onlookers a huge bonfire lit up the night sky and brought the day's celebration to what the spectators all agreed was a fitting conclusion.

The Constitution
of the United States of America

PREAMBLE

We the People of the United States, in order to form a more perfect Union, establish justice, insure domestic tranquility, provide for the common defense, promote the general welfare, and secure the blessings of liberty to ourselves and our posterity, do ordain and establish this Constitution for the United States of America.

ARTICLE I

SECTION ONE
Legislative Power

All legislative powers herein granted shall be vested in a Congress of the United States, which shall consist of a Senate and House of Representatives.

SECTION TWO
House of Representatives, How Constituted, Power of Impeachment

1. The House of Representatives shall be composed of members chosen every second year by the people of the several states, and the electors in each state shall have the qualifications requisite for the electors of the most numerous branch of the state legislature.

2. No person shall be a Representative who shall not have attained to the age of twenty-five years, and been seven years a citizen of the United States, and who shall not, when elected, be an inhabitant of that state in which he shall be chosen.

3. [Representatives and direct taxes shall be apportioned

among the several states which may be included within this Union, according to their respective numbers, which shall be determined by adding to the whole number of free persons, including those bound to service for a term of years, and excluding Indians not taxed, three fifths of all other persons.]* The actual enumeration shall be made within three years after the first meeting of the Congress of the United States, and within every subsequent term of ten years, in such manner as they shall by law direct. The number of Representatives shall not exceed one for every thirty thousand, but each state shall have at least one Representative; and until such enumeration shall be made, the state of New Hampshire shall be entitled to choose three, Massachusetts eight, Rhode Island and Providence Plantations one, Connecticut five, New York six, New Jersey four, Pennsylvania eight, Delaware one, Maryland six, Virginia ten, North Carolina five, South Carolina five, and Georgia three.

4. When vacancies happen in the representation from any state, the executive authority thereof shall issue writs of election to fill such vacancies.

5. The House of Representatives shall choose their speaker and other officers; and shall have the sole power of impeachment.

SECTION THREE
The Senate, How Constituted

1. The Senate of the United States shall be composed of two Senators from each state, [chosen by the legislature thereof,]** for six years; and each Senator shall have one vote.

2. Immediately after they shall be assembled in consequence of the first election, they shall be divided as equally as may be into three classes. The seats of the Senators of the first class shall be vacated at the expiration of the second year, of the second class at the expiration of the fourth year, and of the third class at the expiration of the sixth year, so that one third may be chosen every second year; [and if vacancies happen by resignation, or otherwise, during the recess of the legislature of

*Changed by section 2 of the Fourteenth Amendment, by the Nineteenth Amendment, and by section 1 of the Twenty-sixth Amendment.
**Changed by section 1 of the Seventeenth Amendment.

any state, the executive thereof may make temporary appointments until the next meeting of the legislature, which shall then fill such vacancies.]*

3. No person shall be a Senator who shall not have attained to the age of thirty years, and been nine years a citizen of the United States, and who shall not, when elected, be an inhabitant of that state for which he shall be chosen.

4. The Vice-President of the United States shall be president of the Senate, but shall have no vote unless they be equally divided.

5. The Senate shall choose their other officers, and also a president pro tempore, in the absence of the Vice-President, or when he shall exercise the office of President of the United States.

6. The Senate shall have the sole power to try all impeachments. When sitting for that purpose, they shall be on oath or affirmation. When the President of the United States is tried, the Chief Justice shall preside; and no person shall be convicted without the concurrence of two-thirds of the members present.

7. Judgment in cases of impeachment shall not extend further than to removal from office, and disqualification to hold and enjoy any office of honor, trust, or profit under the United States; but the party convicted shall nevertheless be liable and subject to indictment, trial, judgment, and punishment, according to law.

SECTION FOUR
Election of Senators and Representatives

1. The times, places, and manner of holding elections for Senators and Representatives shall be prescribed in each state by the legislature thereof, but the Congress may at any time by law make or alter such regulations except as to the places of choosing Senators.

2. [The Congress shall assemble at least once in every year, and such meeting shall be on the first Monday in December, unless they shall by law appoint a different day.]**

---

*Changed by section 2 of the Seventeenth Amendment.
**Changed by section 2 of the Twentieth Amendment.

SECTION FIVE
Powers, Quorum, Journals, Meetings, Adjournments

1. Each House shall be the judge of the elections, returns, and qualifications of its own members, and a majority of each shall constitute a quorum to do business; but a smaller number may adjourn from day to day, and may be authorized to compel the attendance of absent members, in such manner, and under such penalties as each House may provide.

2. Each House may determine the rules of its proceedings, punish its members for disorderly behavior, and, with the concurrence of two-thirds, expel a member.

3. Each House shall keep a journal of its proceedings, and from time to time publish the same, excepting such parts as may in their judgment require secrecy; and the yeas and nays of the members of either House on any question shall, at the desire of one-fifth of those present, be entered on the journal.

4. Neither House, during the session of Congress, shall, without the consent of the other, adjourn for more than three days, nor to any other place than that in which the two Houses shall be sitting.

SECTION SIX
Compensation, Privileges, Disabilities

1. The Senators and Representatives shall receive a compensation for their services, to be ascertained by law, and paid out of the Treasury of the United States. They shall in all cases, except treason, felony and breach of the peace, be privileged from arrest during their attendance at the session of their respective Houses, and in going to and returning from the same; and for any speech or debate in either House, they shall not be questioned in any other place.

2. No Senator or Representative shall, during the time for which he was elected, be appointed to any civil office under the authority of the United States, which shall have been created, or the emoluments whereof shall have been increased during such time; and no person holding any office under the United States shall be a member of either House during his continuance in office.

1. All bills for raising revenue shall originate in the House of Representatives; but the Senate may propose or concur with amendments as on other bills.

2. Every bill which shall have passed the House of Representatives and the Senate, shall, before it become a law, be presented to the President of the United States; if he approve he shall sign it, but if not he shall return it, with his objections, to that House in which it shall have originated, who shall enter the objections at large on their journal, and proceed to reconsider it. If after such reconsideration two-thirds of that House shall agree to pass the bill, it shall be sent, together with the objections, to the other House, by which it shall likewise be reconsidered, and if approved by two-thirds of that House, it shall become a law. But in all such cases the votes of both Houses shall be determined by yeas and nays, and the names of the persons voting for and against the bill shall be entered on the journal of each House respectively. If any bill shall not be returned by the President within ten days (Sundays excepted) after it shall have been presented to him, the same shall be a law, in like manner as if he had signed it, unless the Congress by their adjournment prevent its return, in which case it shall not be a law.

3. Every order, resolution, or vote to which the concurrence of the Senate and House of Representatives may be necessary (except on a question of adjournment) shall be presented to the President of the United States; and before the same shall take effect, shall be approved by him, or being disapproved by him, shall be repassed by two-thirds of the Senate and House of Representatives, according to the rules and limitations prescribed in the case of a bill.

SECTION EIGHT
Powers of Congress

The Congress shall have power:

1. To lay and collect taxes, duties, imposts and excises, to pay the debts and provide for the common defense and general

welfare of the United States; but all duties, imposts and excises shall be uniform throughout the United States;

2. To borrow money on the credit of the United States;

3. To regulate commerce with foreign nations, and among the several States, and with the Indian tribes;

4. To establish an uniform rule of naturalization, and uniform laws on the subject of bankruptcies throughout the United States;

5. To coin money, regulate the value thereof, and of foreign coin, and fix the standard of weights and measures;

6. To provide for the punishment of counterfeiting the securities and current coin of the United States;

7. To establish post offices and post roads;

8. To promote the progress of science and useful arts, by securing for limited time to authors and inventors the exclusive right to their respective writings and discoveries;

9. To constitute tribunals inferior to the Supreme Court;

10. To define and punish piracies and felonies committed on the high seas, and offenses against the law of nations;

11. To declare war, grant letter of marque and reprisal, and make rules concerning captures on land and water;

12. To raise and support armies, but no appropriation of money to that use shall be for a longer term than two years;

13. To provide and maintain a navy;

14. To make rules for the government and regulation of the land and naval forces;

15. To provide for calling forth the militia to execute the laws of the Union, suppress insurrections and repel invasions;

16. To provide for organizing, arming and disciplining the militia, and for governing such part of them as may be employed in the service of the United States, reserving to the states respectively, the appointment of the officers, and the authority of training the militia according to the discipline prescribed by Congress;

17. To exercise exclusive legislation in all cases whatsoever, over such district (not exceeding ten miles square) as may, by session of particular states, and the acceptance of Congress, become the seat of the government of the United States, and to exercise like authority over all places purchased by the consent of the legislature of the state in which the same shall be, for the

erection of forts, magazines, arsenals, dock-yards, and other needful buildings; — and

18. To make all laws which shall be necessary and proper for carrying into execution the foregoing powers, and all other powers vested by this Constitution in the Government of the United States, or in any department or officer thereof.

Section Nine
Limitations upon Powers of Congress

1. The migration or importation of such persons as any of the states now existing shall think proper to admit, shall not be prohibited by the Congress prior to the year one thousand eight hundred and eight, but a tax or duty may be imposed on such importation, not exceeding ten dollars for each person.

2. The privilege of the writ of habeas corpus shall not be suspended, unless when in cases of rebellion or invasion the public safety may require it.

3. No bill of attainder or ex post facto law shall be passed.

4. No capitation, or other direct, tax shall be laid, unless in proportion to the census or enumeration herein before directed to be taken.

5. No tax or duty shall be laid on articles exported from any state.

6. No preference shall be given by any regulation of commerce or revenue to the ports of one state over those of another; nor shall vessels bound to, or from, one state, be obliged to enter clear, or pay duties in another.

7. No money shall be drawn from the treasury but in consequence of appropriations made by law; and a regular statement and account of the receipts and expenditures of all public money shall be published from time to time.

8. No title of nobility shall be granted by the United States: And no person holding any office of profit or trust under them, shall, without the consent of the Congress, accept of any present, emolument, office, or title, of any kind whatever from any king, prince, or foreign state.

Section Ten
Restrictions upon Powers of States

1. No state shall enter into any treaty, alliance, or confedera-

tion; grant letters of marque and reprisal; coin money; emit bills of credit; make any thing but gold and silver coin a tender in payment of debts; pass any bill of attainder, ex post facto law, or law impairing the obligation of contracts, or grant any title of nobility.

2. No state shall, without the consent of Congress, lay any imposts or duties on imports or exports, except what may be absolutely necessary for executing its inspection laws; and the net produce of all duties and imposts, laid by any state on imports or exports, shall be for the use of the treasury of the United States; and all such laws shall be subject to the revision and control of the Congress.

3. No state shall, without the consent of Congress, lay any duty of tonnage, keep troops, or ships of war in time of peace, enter into any agreement or compact with another state or with a foreign power, or engage in war, unless actually invaded, or in such imminent danger as will not admit of delay.

ARTICLE II

SECTION ONE
Executive Powers, Electors, Qualifications of the President

1. The executive power shall be vested in a President of the United States of America. He shall hold his office during a term of four years, and, together with the Vice-President, chosen for the same term, be elected, as follows:

2. Each state shall appoint, in such manner as the legislature therefore may direct, a number of electors, equal to the whole number of Senators and Representatives to which the state may be entitled in the Congress; but no Senator or Representative, or person holding an office of trust or profit under the United States, shall be appointed an elector.

3. [The Electors shall meet in their respective states, and vote by ballot for two persons, of whom one at least shall not be an inhabitant of the same state with themselves. And they shall make a list of all the persons voted for, and of the number of votes for each; which list they shall sign and certify, and transmit sealed to the seat of the Government of the United States, directed to the President of the Senate. The President of the Senate shall, in the presence of the Senate and House of Rep-

resentatives, open all the certificates, and the votes shall then be counted. The person having the greatest number of votes shall be the President, if such number be a majority of the whole number of electors appointed; and if there be more than one who have such majority, and have an equal number of votes, then the House of Representatives shall immediately choose by ballot one of them for President; and if no person have a majority, then from the five highest on the list the said House shall in like manner choose the President. But in choosing the President, the votes shall be taken by states, the representation from each state having one vote; a quorum for this purpose shall consist of a member or members from two-thirds of the states, and a majority of all the states shall be necessary to a choice. In every case, after the choice of the President, the person having the greatest number of votes of the electors shall be the Vice-President. But if there should remain two or more who have equal votes, the Senate shall choose from them by ballot the Vice-President.]*

4. The Congress may determine the time of choosing the electors, and the day on which they shall give their votes; which day shall be the same throughout the United States.

5. No person except a natural born citizen, or a citizen of the United States, at the time of the adoption of this Constitution, shall be eligible to the office of President; neither shall any person be eligible to that office who shall not have attained to the age of thirty-five years, and been fourteen years a resident within the United States.

6. [In case of the removal of the President from office, or of his death, resignation, or inability to discharge the powers and duties of the said office, the same shall devolve on the Vice-President, and the Congress may by law provide for the case of removal, death, resignation or inability, both of the President and Vice-President, declaring what officer shall then act as President, and such officer shall act accordingly, until the disability be removed, or a President shall be elected.]**

7. The President shall, at stated times, receive for his services, a compensation, which shall neither be increased nor di-

*Superseded by the Twelfth Amendment.
**Modified by the Twenty-Fifth Amendment.

minished during the period for which he shall have been elected, and he shall not receive within that period any other emolument from the United States, or any of them.

8. Before he enter the execution of this office, he shall take the following oath or affirmation:

"I do solemnly swear (or affirm) that I will faithfully execute the office of President of the United States, and will to the best of my ability, preserve, protect and defend the Constitution of the United States."

SECTION TWO

Powers and Duties of the President

1. The President shall be Commander in Chief of the army and navy of the United States, and of the militia of the several states, when called into the actual service of the United States; he may require the opinion, in writing, of the principal officer in each of the executive departments, upon any subject relating to the duties of their respective offices, and he shall have power to grant reprieves and pardons for offenses against the United States, except in cases of impeachment.

2. He shall have power, by and with the advice and consent of the Senate, to make treaties, provided two-thirds of the Senators present concur; and he shall nominate, and by and with the advice and consent of the Senate, shall appoint ambassadors, other public ministers and consuls, judges of the Supreme Court, and all other officers of the United States, whose appointments are not herein otherwise provided for, and which shall be established by law; but the Congress may by law vest the appointment of such inferior officers, as they think proper, in the President alone, in the courts of law, or in the heads of departments.

3. The President shall have power to fill up all vacancies that may happen during the recess of the Senate, by granting commissions which shall expire at the end of their next session.

SECTION THREE

Additional Powers and Duties of the President

He shall from time to time give to the Congress information of the state of the Union, and recommend to their consideration such measures as he shall judge necessary and expedient; he may, on extraordinary occasions, convene both Houses, or either of them, and in case of disagreement between them, with respect to the time of adjournment, he may adjourn them to such time as he shall think proper; he shall receive ambassadors and other public ministers; he shall take care that the laws be faithfully executed, and shall commission all the officers of the United States.

SECTION FOUR
Forfeiture of Offices for Crimes

The President, Vice-President and all civil officers of the United States, shall be removed from office on impeachment for, and conviction of, treason, bribery, or other crimes and misdemeanors.

ARTICLE III

SECTION ONE
Judicial Powers, Tenure of Office

The judicial power of the United States, shall be vested in one Supreme Court, and in such inferior courts as the Congress may from time to time ordain and establish. The judges, both of the Supreme and inferior courts, shall hold their offices during good behavior, and shall, at stated times, receive for their services a compensation, which shall not be diminished during their continuance in office.

SECTION TWO
Cases to Which Judicial Power Extends

1. The judicial power shall extend to all cases, in law and equity, arising under this Constitution, the laws of the United States, and treaties made, or which shall be made, under their authority; − to all cases affecting ambassadors, other public ministers and consuls; − to all cases of admiralty and maritime jurisdiction; − to controversies to which the United States shall be a party; − to controversies between two or more states; − between a state and citizens of another state; − between citizens of different states; − between citizens of the same state

claiming lands under grants of different states, and between a state, or the citizens thereof, and foreign states, citizens or subjects.

2. In all cases affecting ambassadors, other public ministers and consuls, and those in which a state shall be party, the Supreme Court shall have original jurisdiction. In all the other cases before mentioned, the Supreme Court shall have appellate jurisdiction, both as to law and fact, with such exceptions, and under such regulations as the Congress shall make.

3. The trial of all crimes, except in cases of impeachment, shall be by jury; and such trial shall be held in the state where said crimes shall have been committed; but when not committed within any state, the trial shall be at such place or places as the Congress may by law have directed.

SECTION THREE
Treason, Proof, and Punishment

1. Treason against the United States, shall consist only in levying war against them, or in adhering to their enemies, giving them aid and comfort. No person shall be convicted of treason unless on the testimony of two witnesses to the same overt act, or on confession in open court.

2. The Congress shall have power to declare the punishment of treason, but no attainder of treason shall work corruption of blood or forfeiture except during the life of the person attained.

ARTICLE IV

SECTION ONE
Faith and Credit among States

Full faith and credit shall be given in each state to the public acts, records, and judicial proceedings of every other state. And the Congress may by general laws prescribe the manner in which such acts, records and proceedings shall be proved, and the effect thereof.

SECTION TWO
Surrender of Fugitives

1. The citizens of each state shall be entitled to all privileges

and immunities of citizens in the several states.

2. A person charged in any state with treason, felony, or other crime, who shall flee from justice, and be found in another state, shall on demand of the executive authority of the state, from which he fled, be delivered up, to be removed to the state having jurisdiction of the crime.

3. [No person held to service or labor in one state, under the laws thereof, escaping into another, shall, in consequence of any law or regulation therein, be discharged from such service or labor, but shall be delivered up on claim of the party to whom such service of labor may be due.]*

SECTION THREE
Admission of New States

1. New states may be admitted by the Congress into this Union, but no new state shall be formed or erected within the jurisdiction of any other state; nor any state be formed by the junction of two or more states, or parts of states, without the consent of the legislatures of the states concerned as well as of the Congress.

2. The Congress shall have power to dispose of and make all needful rules and regulation respecting the territory or other property belonging to the United States, and nothing in this Constitution shall be so construed as to prejudice any claims of the United States, or of any particular state.

SECTION FOUR
Guarantee of Republican Government

The United States shall guarantee to every state in this Union a republican form of government, and shall protect each of them against invasion; and on application of the legislature, or of the executive (when the legislature cannot be convened) against domestic violence.

ARTICLE V

Amendment of the Constitution

---

*Superseded by the Thirteenth Amendment.

The Congress, whenever two-thirds of both Houses shall deem it necessary, shall propose amendments to this Constitution, or, on the application of the legislatures of two-thirds of the several states, shall call a convention for proposing amendments, which, in either case, shall be valid to all intents and purposes, as part of this Constitution, when ratified by the legislatures of three-fourths of the several states, or by conventions in three-fourths thereof, as the one or the other mode of ratification may be proposed by the Congress; provided that no amendment which may be made prior to the year one thousand eight hundred and eight shall in any manner affect the first and fourth clauses in the ninth section of the first article; and that no state, without its consent, shall be deprived of its equal suffrage in the Senate.

ARTICLE VI
Miscellaneous Provisions

1. All debts contracted and engagements entered into, before the adoption of this Constitution, shall be valid against the United States under this Constitution, as under the confederation.

2. This Constitution, and the laws of the United States which shall be made in pursuance thereof; and all treaties made, or which shall be made, under the authority of the United States, shall be the supreme law of the land; and the judges in every state shall be bound thereby, anything in the Constitution or laws or any state to the contrary notwithstanding.

3. The Senators and Representatives before mentioned, and the members of the several state legislatures, and all executive and judicial officers, both of the United States and of the several states, shall be bound by oath or affirmation, to support this Constitution; but no religious test shall ever be required as a qualification to any office of public trust under the United States.

ARTICLE VII
Ratification and Establishment

The ratification of the conventions of nine states, shall be sufficient for the establishment of this Constitution between the states so ratifying the same.

Done in convention by the Unanimous Consent of the States present the Seventeenth Day of September in the Year of our Lord one thousand seven hundred and Eighty seven and of the Independence of the United States of America the Twelfth In Witness whereof We have hereunto subscribed our Names,

G⁰ Washington-Presid⁺

and deputy from Virginia

SIGNERS OF THE CONSTITUTION

CONNECTICUT
  William Samuel Johnson
  Roger Sherman
GEORGIA
  Abraham Baldwin
  William Few
MARYLAND
  Daniel Carroll
  Daniel Jenifer
  James McHenry
MASSACHUSETTS
  Nathaniel Gorham
  Rufus King
NEW HAMPSHIRE
  Nicholas Gilman
  John Langdon
NEW JERSEY
  David Brearly
  Jonathan Dayton
  William Livingston
  William Paterson
NEW YORK
  Alexander Hamilton
NORTH CAROLINA
  William Blount
  Richard Dodds Spaight
  Hugh Williamson

DELAWARE
  Richard Bassett
  Gunning Bedford, Jr.
  Jacob Broom
  John Dickinson
  George Read
PENNSYLVANIA
  George Clymer
  Thomas FitzSimons
  Benjamin Franklin
  Jared Ingersoll
  Thomas Mifflin
  Gouverneur Morris
  Robert Morris
  James Wilson
RHODE ISLAND
  None
SOUTH CAROLINA
  Pierce Butler
  Charles Pinckney
  Charles Cotesworth
    Pinckney
  John Rutledge
VIRGINIA
  John Blair
  James Madison
  George Washington

This Constitution was adopted on September 17, 1787 by the Constitutional Convention, and was declared ratified on July 2, 1788.

Amendments to the Constitution

Since 1787, twenty-six amendments have been proposed by the Congress and ratified by the several states, pursuant to the fifth Article of the original Constitution.

ARTICLE I

Congress shall make no law respecting an establishment of religion, or prohibiting the free exercise thereof; or abridging the freedom of speech, or of the press; or the right of the people peaceably to assemble, and to petition the Government for a redress of grievances.

ARTICLE II

A well regulated Militia, being necessary to the security of a free State, the right of the people to keep and bear Arms, shall not be infringed.

ARTICLE III

No Soldier shall, in time of peace be quartered in any house without the consent of the Owner, nor in time of war, but in a manner to be prescribed by law.

ARTICLE IV

The right of the people to be secure in their persons, houses, papers, and effects, against unreasonable searches and seizures, shall not be violated, and no Warrants shall issue, but upon probable cause, supported by Oath or affirmation, and particularly describing the place to be searched, and the persons or things to be seized.

ARTICLE V

No person shall be held to answer for a capital, or otherwise infamous crime, unless on a presentment or indictment of a Grand Jury, except in cases arising in the land or naval forces, or in the Militia, when in actual service in time of War or public danger; nor shall any person be subject for the same offence to be twice put in jeopardy of life or limb; nor shall be compelled in any criminal case to be a witness against himself, nor be deprived of life, liberty, or property, without due process of law; nor shall private property be taken for public use, without just compensation.

ARTICLE VI

In all criminal prosecutions, the accused shall enjoy the right to a speedy and public trial, by an impartial jury of the State and district wherein the crime shall have been committed, which district shall have been previously ascertained by law, and to be informed of the nature and cause of the accusation; to be confronted with the witnesses against him; to have compulsory process for obtaining witnesses in his favor, and to have the Assistance of Counsel for his defence.

ARTICLE VII

In Suits at common law, where the value in controversy shall exceed twenty dollars, the right of trial by jury shall be preserved, and no fact tried by a jury, shall be otherwise re-examined in any Court of the United States, than according to the rules of the common law.

ARTICLE VIII

Excessive bail shall not be required, nor excessive fines imposed, nor cruel and unusual punishment inflicted.

ARTICLE IX

The enumeration in the Constitution, of certain rights shall not be construed to deny or disparage others retained by the people.

ARTICLE X

The powers not delegated to the United States by the Constitution, nor prohibited by it to the States, are reserved to the States respectively, or to the people.

ARTICLE XI

The Judicial power of the United States shall not be construed to extend to any suit in law or equity, commenced or prosecuted against one of the United States by Citizens of another State, or by Citizens or Subjects of any Foreign State.

ARTICLE XII

The Electors shall meet in their respective states, and vote by ballot for President and Vice-President, one of whom, at least, shall not be an inhabitant of the same state with themselves; they shall name in their ballots the person voted for as President, and in distinct ballots the person voted for as Vice-President, and they shall make distinct lists of all persons voted for as President, and of all persons voted for as Vice-President, and of the number of votes for each, which lists they shall sign and certify, and transmit sealed to the seat of the government of the United States, directed to the President of the Senate; − The President of the Senate shall, in the presence of the Senate and House of Representatives, open all the certificates and the votes shall then be counted; − The person having the greatest number of votes for President, shall be the President, if such number be a majority of the whole number of Electors appointed; and if no person have such majority, then from the persons having the highest numbers not exceeding three on the list of those voted for as President, the House of Representatives shall choose immediately, by ballot, the President. But in choosing the President, the votes shall be taken by states, the representation from each state having one vote; a quorum for this purpose shall consist of a member or members from two-thirds of the states, and a majority of all the states shall be necessary to a choice.

And if the House of Representatives shall not choose a President whenever the right of choice shall devolve upon them, before the fourth day of March next following, then the Vice-President shall act as President, as in the case of the death or other constitutional disability of the President. The person having the greatest number of votes as Vice-President, shall be the Vice-President, if such number be a majority of the whole number of Electors appointed, and if no person have a majority, then from the two highest numbers on the list, the Senate shall choose the Vice-President; a quorum for the purpose shall consist of two-thirds of the whole number of Senators, and a majority of the whole number shall be necessary to a choice. But no person constitutionally ineligible to the office of President shall be eligible to that of Vice-President of the United States.

ARTICLE XIII

Section 1. Neither slavery nor involuntary servitude, except as a punishment for crime whereof the party shall have been duly convicted, shall exist within the United States, or any place subject to their jurisdiction.

Section 2. Congress shall have power to enforce this article by appropriate legislation.

ARTICLE XIV

Section 1. All persons born or naturalized in the United States, and subject to the jurisdiction thereof, are citizens of the United States and of the State wherein they reside. No State shall make or enforce any law which shall abridge the privileges or immunities of citizens of the United States; nor shall any State deprive any person of life, liberty, or property, without due process of law; nor deny to any person within its jurisdiction the equal protection of the laws.

Section 2. Representatives shall be apportioned among the several States according to their respective numbers, counting the whole number of persons in each State, excluding Indians not taxed. But when the right to vote at any election for the choice of electors for President and Vice President of the United States, Representatives in Congress, the Executive and Judicial officers of a State, or the members of the Legislature thereof, is denied to any of the male inhabitants of such State, being twenty-one years of age, and citizens of the United States, or in any way abridged, except for participation in rebellion, or other crime, the basis of representation therein shall be reduced in the proportion which the number of such male citizens shall bear to the whole number of male citizens twenty-one years of age in such State.

Section 3. No person shall be a Senator or Representative in Congress, or elector of President and Vice-President, or hold any office, civil or military, under the United States, or under any State, who, having previously taken an oath, as a member of Congress, or as an officer of the United States, or as a member of any State legislature, or as an executive or judicial officer of any State, to support the Constitution of the United States, shall have engaged in insurrection or rebellion against the same, or given aid or comfort to the enemies thereof. But Congress may by a vote of two-thirds of each House, remove such disability.

Section 4. The validity of the public debt of the United States, authorized by law, including debts incurred for payment of pensions and bounties for services in suppressing insurrection or rebellion, shall not be questioned. But neither the United States nor any State shall assume or pay any debt or obligation incurred in aid of insurrection or rebellion against the United States, or any claim for the loss or emancipation of any slave; but all such debts, obligations and claims shall be held illegal and void.

Section 5. The Congress shall have power to enforce, by appropriate legislation, the provisions of this article.

ARTICLE XV

Section 1. The right of citizens of the United States to vote shall not be denied or abridged by the United States or by any State on account of race, color, or previous condition of servitude.

Section 2. The Congress shall have power to enforce this article by appropriate legislation.

ARTICLE XVI

The Congress shall have power to lay and collect taxes on incomes, from whatever source derived, without apportionment among the several States, and without regard to any census or enumeration.

ARTICLE XVII

The Senate of the United States shall be composed of two Senators from each State, elected by the people thereof, for six years; and each Senator shall have one vote. The electors in each State shall have the qualifications requisite for electors of the most numerous branch of the State legislatures.

When vacancies happen in the representation of any State in the Senate, the executive authority of such State shall issue writs of election to fill such vacancies: *Provided*, That the legislature of any State may empower the executive thereof to make temporary appointments until the people fill the vacancies by election as the legislature may direct.

This amendment shall not be so construed as to affect the election or term of any Senator chosen before it becomes valid as part of the Constitution.

ARTICLE XVIII

[Section 1. After one year from the ratification of this article the manufacture, sale, or transportation of intoxicating liquors within, the importation thereof into, or the exportation thereof from the United States and all territory subject to the jurisdiction thereof for beverage purposes is hereby prohibited.

[Section 2. The Congress and Several States shall have concurrent power to enforce this article by appropriate legislation.

[Section 3. This article shall be inoperative unless it shall have been ratified as an amendment to the Constitution by the legislatures of the several States, as provided in the Constitution, within seven years from the date of the submission hereof to the States by the Congress.]

ARTICLE XIX

The right of citizens of the United States to vote shall not be denied or abridged by the United States or by any State on account of sex.

Congress shall have power to enforce this article by appropriate legislation.

ARTICLE XX

Section 1. The terms of the President and Vice President shall end at noon on the 20th day of January, and the terms of Senators and Representatives at noon on the 3d day of January, of the years in which such terms would have ended if this article had not been ratified; and the terms of their successors shall then begin.

Section 2. The Congress shall assemble at least once in every year, and such meeting shall begin at noon on the 3d day of January, unless they shall by law appoint a different day.

Section 3. If, at the time fixed for the beginning of the term of the President, the President elect shall have died, the Vice President elect shall become President. If a President shall not have been chosen before the time fixed for the beginning of his term, or if the President elect shall have failed to qualify, then the Vice President elect shall act as President until a President shall have qualified; and the Congress may by law provide for the case wherein neither a President elect nor a Vice President elect shall have qualified, declaring who shall then act as President, or the manner in which one who is to act shall be selected, and such person shall act accordingly until a President or Vice President shall have qualified.

Section 4. The Congress may by law provide for the case of the death of any of the persons from whom the House of Representatives may choose a President whenever the right of choice shall have devolved upon them, and for the case of the death of any of the persons from whom the Senate may choose a Vice President whenever the right of choice shall have devolved upon them.

Section 5. Sections 1 and 2 shall take effect on the 15th day of October following the ratification of this article.

Section 6. This article shall be inoperative unless it shall have been ratified as an amendment to the Constitution by the legislatures of three-fourths of the several States within seven years from the date of its submission.

ARTICLE XXI

Section 1. The eighteenth article of amendment to the Constitution of the United States is hereby repealed.

Section 2. The transportation or importation into any State, Territory, or possession of the United States for delivery or use therein of intoxicating liquors, in violation of the laws thereof, is hereby prohibited.

Section 3. This article shall be inoperative unless it shall have been ratified as an amendment to the Constitution by conventions in the several States, as provided in the Constitution, within seven years from the date of the submission hereof to the States by the Congress.

ARTICLE XXII

Section 1. No person shall be elected to the office of the President more than twice, and no person who has held the office of President, or acted as President, for more than two years of a term to which some other person was elected President shall be elected to the office of the President more than once. But this Article shall not apply to any person holding the office of President when this Article was proposed by the Congress, and shall not prevent any person who may be holding the office of President, or acting as President, during the term within which this Article becomes operative from holding the office of President or acting as President during the remainder of such term.

Section 2. This article shall be inoperative unless it shall have been ratified as an amendment to the Constitution by the legislatures of three-fourths of the several States within seven years from the date of its submission to the States by the Congress.

ARTICLE XXIII

Section 1. The District constituting the seat of Government of the United States shall appoint in such manner as the Congress may direct:

A number of electors of President and Vice President equal to the whole number of Senators and Representatives in Congress to which the District would be entitled if it were a State, but in no event more than the least populous State; they shall be in addition to those appointed by the States, but they shall be considered, for the purposes of the election of President and Vice President, to be electors appointed by a State; and they shall meet in the District and perform such duties as provided by the twelfth article amendment.

Section 2. The Congress shall have power to enforce this article by appropriate legislation.

ARTICLE XXIV

Section 1. The right of citizens of the United States to vote in any primary or other election for President or Vice President, for electors for President or Vice President, or for Senator or Representative in Congress, shall not be denied or abridged by the United States or any State by reason of failure to pay any poll tax or other tax.

Section 2. The Congress shall have power to enforce this article by appropriate legislation.

ARTICLE XXV

Section 1. In case of removal of the President from office or of his death or resignation, the Vice President shall become President.

Section 2. Whenever there is a vacancy in the office of the Vice President, the President shall nominate a Vice President who shall take office upon confirmation by a majority vote of both Houses of Congress.

Section 3. Whenever the President transmits to the President pro tempore of the Senate and the Speaker of the House of Representatives his written declaration that he is unable to discharge the powers and duties of his office, and until he transmits to them a written declaration to the contrary, such powers and duties shall be discharged by the Vice President as Acting President.

Section 4. Whenever the Vice President and a majority of either the principal officers of the executive departments or of such other body as Congress may by law provide, transmit to the President pro tempore of the Senate and the Speaker of the

House of Representatives their written declaration that the President is unable to discharge the powers and duties of his office, the Vice President shall immediately assume the powers and duties of the office as Acting President.

Thereafter, when the President transmits to the President pro tempore of the Senate and the Speaker of the House of Representatives his written declaration that no inability exists, he shall resume the powers and duties of his office unless the Vice President and a majority of either the principal officers of the executive department or of such other body as Congress may by law provide, transmit within four days to the President pro tempore of the Senate and the Speaker of the House of Representatives their written declaration that the President is unable to discharge the powers and duties of his office. Thereupon Congress shall decide the issue, assembling within forty-eight hours for that purpose if not in session. If the Congress, within twenty-one days after receipt of the latter written declaration, or, if Congress is not in session, within twenty-one days after Congress is required to assemble, determines by two-thirds vote of both Houses that the President is unable to discharge the powers and duties of his office, the Vice President shall continue to discharge the same as Acting President; otherwise, the President shall resume the powers and duties of his office.

ARTICLE XXVI

Section 1. The right of citizens of the United States, who are eighteen years of age or older, to vote shall not be denied or abridged by the United States or by any State on account of age.

Section 2. The Congress shall have power to enforce this article by appropriate legislation.

Delegates to the Massachusetts Ratifying Convention*

COUNTY OF SUFFOLK.

Boston, ...	His Excellency John Hancock, Esq.
	Hon. James Bowdoin, Esq.
	Hon. Samuel Adams, Esq.
	Hon. William Phillips, Esq.
	Hon. Caleb Davis, Esq.
	Charles Jarvis, Esq.
	John Coffin Jones, Esq.
	John Winthrop, Esq.
	Thomas Dawes, Jr., Esq.
	Rev. Samuel Stillman.
	Thomas Russell, Esq.
	Christopher Gore, Esq.
Roxbury, ...	Hon. William Heath, Esq.
	Hon. Increase Sumner, Esq.
Dorchester, ...	James Bowdoin, Jr., Esq.
	Ebenezer Wales, Esq.
Milton, ...	Rev. Nathaniel Robbins.
Weymouth, ...	Hon. Cotton Tufts, Esq.
Hingham, ...	Hon. Benjamin Lincoln, Esq.
	Rev. Daniel Shute.

*The list of delegates is derived from "A Journal of a Convention of Delegates, chosen by the people of the Commonwealth of Massachusetts, for the purpose of considering a constitution or frame of government, reported by a convention of delegates, held at Philadelphia, on the first Monday of May, 1787" in *Debates and Proceedings in the Convention of the Commonwealth of Massachusetts, held in the year 1788, and which finally ratified the Constitution of the United States.* Boston, William White, 1856.

Braintree, ... Hon. Richard Cranch, Esq.
Rev. Anthony Wibird.
Brookline, ... Rev. Joseph Jackson.
Dedham, ... Rev. Thomas Thacher.
Fisher Ames, Esq.
Needham, ... Col. William McIntosh.
Medfield, ... Capt. John Baxter, Jr.
Stoughton, ... Hon. Elijah Dunbar, Esq.
Capt. Jedidiah Southworth.
Wrentham, ... Mr. Thomas Mann.
Mr. Nathan Comstock.
Walpole, ... Mr. George Payson.
Sharon, ... Mr. Benjamin Randall.
Cohasset, ...
Franklin, ... Hon. Jabez Fisher, Esq.
Medway, ... Mr. Moses Richardson, Jr.
Bellingham, ... Rev. Noah Alden.
Hull, ... Mr. Thomas Jones.
Chelsea, ... Rev. Phillips Payson.
Foxborough, ... Mr. Ebenezer Warren.

COUNTY OF ESSEX.

Salem, ... Richard Manning, Esq.
Edward Pulling, Esq.
Mr. William Gray, Esq.
Mr. Francis Cabot.
Danvers, ... Hon. Samuel Holten, Esq.
Hon. Israel Hutchinson, Esq.
Newbury, ... Hon. Tristram Dalton, Esq.
Enoch Sawyer, Esq.
Ebenezer March, Esq.
Newbury Port, . . . Hon. Rufus King, Esq.
Hon. Benjamin Greenleaf, Esq.
Theophilus Parsons, Esq.
Hon. Jonathan Titcomb, Esq.
Beverly, ... Hon. George Cabot, Esq.
Mr. Joseph Wood.
Capt. Israel Thorndike.

Ipswich, ...	Hon. Michael Farley, Esq.
	John Choate, Esq.
	Daniel Noyes, Esq.
	Col. Jonathan Cogswell.
Marblehead, ...	Isaac Mansfield, Esq.
	Jonathan Glover, Esq.
	Hon. Azor Orne, Esq.
	John Glover, Esq.
Gloucester, ...	Daniel Rogers, Esq.
	John Low, Esq.
	Capt. William Pearson.
Lynn and ⎫	⎧ John Carnes, Esq.
Lynnfield, ⎭ . . .	⎩ Capt. John Burnham.
Andover, ...	Capt. Peter Osgood, Jr.
	Dr. Thomas Kittridge.
	Mr. William Symmes, Jr.
Rowley, ...	Capt. Thomas Mighill.
Haverhill, ...	Bailey Bartlett, Esq.
	Capt. Nathaniel Marsh.
Topsfield, ...	Mr. Israel Clark.
Salisbury, ...	Dr. Samuel Nye.
	Mr. Enoch Jackman.
Almsbury, ...	Capt. Benjamin Lurvey.
	Mr. Willis Patten.
Boxford, ...	Hon. Aaron Wood, Esq.
Bradford, ...	Daniel Thurston, Esq.
Methuen, ...	Capt. Ebenezer Carlton.
Wenham, ...	Mr. Jacob Herrick.
Manchester, ...	Mr. Simeon Miller.
Middleton, ...	

COUNTY OF MIDDLESEX.

Cambridge, ...	Hon. Francis Dana, Esq.
	Stephen Dana, Esq.
Charlestown, ...	Hon. Nathaniel Gorham, Esq.
Watertown, ...	Dr. Marshall Spring.
Woburn, ...	Capt. Timothy Winn.
	Mr. James Fowle, Jr.
Concord, ...	Hon. Joseph Hosmer, Esq.
Newton, ...	Hon. Abraham Fuller, Esq.

Reading, ...	Mr. William Flint.
	Mr. Peter Emerson.
Marlborough, . . .	Mr. Jonas Morse.
	Maj. Benjamin Sawin.
Billerica, ...	William Tompson, Esq.
Framingham, ...	Capt. Lawson Buckminster.
Lexington, ...	Benjamin Brown, Esq.
Chelmsford, ...	Maj. John Minot.
Sherburne, ...	Daniel Whitney, Esq.
Sudbury, ...	Capt. Asahel Wheeler.
Malden, ...	Capt. Benjamin Blaney.
Weston, ...	Capt. Abraham Bigelow.
Medford, ...	Maj. Gen. John Brooks.
Hopkinton, ...	Capt. Gilbert Dench.
Westford, ...	Mr. Jonathan Keep.
Stow, ...	Dr. Charles Whitman.
Groton, ...	Dr. Benjamin Morse.
	Joseph Sheple, Esq.
Shirley, ...	Mr. Obadiah Sawtell.
Pepperell, ...	Mr. Daniel Fisk.
Waltham, ...	Leonard Williams, Esq.
Townshend, ...	Capt. Daniel Adams.
Dracut, ...	Hon. Joseph Bradley Varnum, Esq.
Bedford, ...	Capt. John Webber.
Holliston, ...	Capt. Staples Chamberlin.
Acton and Carlisle, . .	Mr. Asa Parlin.
Dunstable, ...	Hon. John Pitts, Esq.
Lincoln, ...	Hon. Eleazer Brooks, Esq.
Wilmington, ...	Capt. John Harnden.
Tewksbury, . . .	Mr. Newman Scarlett.
Littleton, ...	Mr. Samuel Reed.
Ashby, ...	Mr. Benjamin Adams.
Natick, ...	Maj. Hezekiah Broad.
Stoneham, ...	Capt. Jonathan Green.
East Sudbury, . . .	Mr. Phineas Gleazen.

COUNTY OF HAMPSHIRE.[1]

Boxborough, ...	
Springfield, . . .	. William Pynchon, Esq.
West Springfield, .	. Col. Benjamin Ely.
	Capt. John Williston.
Wilbraham, ...	. Capt. Phinehas Stebbins.
Northampton and	{ Hon. Caleb Strong, Esq.
Easthampton, . .	{ Mr. Benjamin Sheldon.
Southampton, . .	. Capt. Lemuel Pomeroy.
Hadley, ...	. Brig. Gen. Elisha Porter.
Southadley, . . .	. Hon. Noah Goodman, Esq.
Amherst, ...	. Mr. Daniel Cooley.
Granby, ...	. Mr. Benjamin Eastman.
Hatfield, ...	. Hon. John Hastings, Esq.
Whately, ...	. Mr. Josiah Allis.
Williamsburg, . .	. Mr. William Bodman.
Westfield, ...	. John Ingersoll, Esq.
	Mr. John Phelps.
Deerfield, ...	. Mr. Samuel Field.
Greenfield, . . .	. Mr. Moses Bascom.
Shelburne, ...	. Mr. Robert Wilson.
Conway, ...	. Capt. Consider Arms.
	Mr. Malachi Maynard.
Sunderland, . . .	. Capt. Zacheus Crocker.
Montague, ...	. Mr. Moses Severance.
Northfield, . . .	. Mr. Ebenezer Janes.
Brimfield, ...	. Abner Morgan, Esq.
South Brimfield, . .	. Capt. Asa Fisk.
Monson, ...	. Mr. Phinehas Merrick.
Pelham, ...	. Mr. Adam Clark.
Greenwich, . . .	. Capt. Nathaniel Whitcomb.
Blanford, ...	. Mr. Timothy Blair.
Palmer, ...	. Mr. Aaron Merrick.
Granville, ...	. Mr. John Hamilton.
	Mr. Clark Cooley.
New Salem, . . .	. Mr. John Chamberlin.

[1][Hampshire County, in 1788, included the present counties of Hampshire, Hampden and Franklin.]

Belchertown, ...	. Mr. Justus Dwight.
Colrain, ...	. Mr. Samuel Eddy.
Ware, ...	. Mr. Isaac Pepper.
Warwick and } . .	. Capt. John Goldsbury.
Orange,	
Bernardston	. Capt. Agrippa Wells.
Chester, ...	. Capt. David Shepard.
Charlemont, . . .	. Mr. Jesse Reed.
Ashfield, ...	. Mr. Ephraim William.
Worthington, . . .	. Nahum Eager, Esq.
Shutesbury, . . .	. Mr. Asa Powers.
Chesterfield, . . .	. Col. Benjamin Bonney.
Goshen, ...	.
Southwick, . . .	. Capt. Silas Fowler.
Norwich, ...	. Maj. Thomas James Douglass.
Ludlow, ...	. Mr. John Jennings.
Leverett, ...	. Mr. Jonathan Hubbard.
Westhampton, . .	. Mr. Aaron Fisher.
Montgomery, . . .	.
Cummington and } .	Mr. Edmund Lazell.
Plainfield,	
Buckland, ...	. Capt. Thompson Maxwell.
Longmeadow, . . .	. Mr. Elihu Colton.
Middlefield, . . .	.
Wendell, ...	.

COUNTY OF PLYMOUTH.

Plymouth, ...	. Joshua Thomas, Esq.
	Mr. Thomas Davis.
	Mr. John Davis.
Scituate, ...	. Hon. William Cushing, Esq.
	Hon. Nathan Cushing, Esq.
	Hon. Charles Turner, Esq.
Duxborough, . . .	. Hon. George Partridge, Esq.
Marshfield, . . .	. Rev. William Shaw.
Bridgwater, . . .	. Daniel Howard, Esq.
	Mr. Hezekiah Hooper.
	Capt. Elisha Mitchell.
	Mr. Daniel Howard, Jr.

Middleborough, . . .	Rev. Isaac Backus.
	Mr. Benjamin Thomas.
	Isaac Tomson, Esq.
	Mr. Isaac Soul.
Rochester, ...	Mr. Nathaniel Hammond.
	Mr. Abraham Holmes.
Plympton, ...	Capt. Francis Shurtliff.
	Mr. Elijah Bisbee, Jr.
Pembroke, ...	Capt. John Turner.
	Mr. Josiah Smith.
Kingston, ...	William Sever, Jr., Esq.
Hanover, ...	Hon. Joseph Cushing, Esq.
Abington, ...	Rev. Samuel Niles.
Halifax, ...	Mr. Freman Waterman.
Wareham, ...	Col. Israel Fearing.

COUNTY OF BARNSTABLE.

Barnstable, . . .	Nymphas Marston, Esq.
	Shearjashub Bourn, Esq.
Sandwich, ...	Dr. Thomas Smith.
	Mr. Thomas Nye.
Yarmouth, ...	David Thacher, Esq.
	Capt. Jonathan Howes.
Eastham, ...	
Harwich, ...	Hon. Solomon Freeman, Esq.
	Capt. Kimbal Clark.
Welfleet, ...	Rev. Levi Whitman.
Falmouth, ...	Capt. Joseph Palmer.
Truro, ...	
Chatham, ...	
Province Town, . . .	

COUNTY OF BRISTOL.

Taunton, ...	James Williams, Esq.
	Col. Nathaniel Leonard.
	Mr. Aaron Pratt.
Rehoboth, ...	Capt. Phanuel Bishop.
	Maj. Frederick Drown.
Rehoboth, ...	William Winsor, Esq.

Swanzey, ...	Mr. Christopher Mason.
	Mr. David Brown.
Dartmouth, ...	Hon. Holder Slocum, Esq.
	Mr. Meletiah Hathaway.
Norton, ...	Hon. Abraham White, Esq.
Attleborough, ...	Hon. Elisha May, Esq.
	Capt. Moses Willmarth.
Dighton, ...	Col. Sylvester Richmond.
	Hon. William Baylies, Esq.
Freetown, ...	Hon. Thomas Durfee, Esq.
	Mr. Richard Bordon.
Rainham, ...	Israel Washburn, Esq.
Easton, ...	Capt. Ebenezer Tisdell.
Mansfield, ...	Capt. John Pratt.
Berkley, ...	Samuel Tobey, Esq.
New Bedford, . . .	Hon. Walter Spooner, Esq.
	Rev. Samuel West.
Westport, ...	Mr. William Almy.

COUNTY OF YORK.[2]

York, ...	Capt. Esaias Preble.
	Nathaniel Barrell, Esq.
Kittery, ...	Mr. Mark Adams.
	Mr. James Neal.
Wells, ...	Rev. Dr. Moses Hemmenway.
	Hon. Nathaniel Wells, Esq.
Berwick, ...	Capt. Elijah Thayer.
	Dr. Nathaniel Low.
	Mr. Richard Fox Cutts.
Arundell, ...	
Biddeford, ...	
Pepperellboro', . . .	Thomas Cutts, Esq.
Lebanon, ...	Mr. Thomas M. Wentworth.
Sanford, ...	Maj. Samuel Nasson.
Buxton, ...	Jacob Bradbury, Esq.
Fryeburg, ...	Mr. Moses Ames.
Coxhall, ...	Capt. John Low.

[2][In the present State of Maine.]

Massabeseck, ...
Limerick, ...
Brownfield, ...
Little Falls, ...
Shapleigh, ... Mr. Jeremiah Emery.
Pearsonfield, ...
Waterborough, . . . Rev. Pelatiah Tingley.

COUNTY OF DUKES COUNTY.

Edgartown, ... Mr. William Mayhew.
Chilmark, ...
Tisbury, ... Mr. Cornelius Dunham.

COUNTY OF NANTUCKET.

Sherburne, ...

COUNTY OF WORCESTER.

Worcester, ... Hon. Samuel Curtis, Esq.
　　　　　　　　　　Mr. David Bigelow.
Lancaster, ... Hon. John Sprague, Esq.
Mendon, ... Edward Thompson, Esq.
Brookfield, ... Mr. James Nichols.
　　　　　　　　　　Mr. Daniel Forbes.
　　　　　　　　　　Mr. Nathaniel Jenks.
Oxford, ... Capt. Jeremiah Learned.
Charlton, ... Mr. Caleb Curtis.
　　　　　　　　　　Mr. Ezra McIntier.
Sutton, ... Mr. David Harwood.
　　　　　　　　　　Hon. Amos Singletary, Esq.
Leicester, ... Col. Samuel Denny.
Spencer, ... Mr. James Hathaway.
Rutland, ... Mr. Asaph Sherman.
Paxton, ... Mr. Abraham Smith.
Oakham, ... Capt. Jonathan Bullard.
Barre, ... Capt. John Black.
Hubbardston, ... Capt. John Woods.
New Braintree, . . . Capt. Benjamin Josselyn.
Southborough, . . . Capt. Seth Newton.
Westborough, ... Capt. Stephen Maynard.

Northborough, . . . Mr. Artemas Brigham.
Shrewsbury, ... Capt. Isaac Harrington.
Lunenburgh, ... Capt. John Fuller.
Fitchburgh, ... Mr. Daniel Putnam.
Uxbridge, ... Dr. Samuel Willard.
Harvard, ... Josiah Whitney, Esq.
Dudley, ... Mr. Jonathan Day.
Bolton, ... Hon. Samuel Baker, Esq.
Upton, ... Capt. Thomas M. Baker.
Sturbridge, ... Capt. Timothy Parker.
Leominster, ... Maj. David Wilder.
Hardwick, ... Maj. Martin Kinsley.
Holden, ... Rev. Joseph Davis.
Western, ... Mr. Matthew Patrick.
Douglass, ... Hon. John Taylor, Esq.
Grafton, ... Dr. Joseph Wood.
Petersham, ... Jonathan Grout, Esq.
                       Capt. Samuel Peckham.
Royalston, ... John Frye, Esq.
Westminster, ... Mr. Stephen Holden.
Templeton, ... Capt. Joel Fletcher.
Princeton, ... Mr. Timothy Fuller.
Ashburnham, . . . Mr. Jacob Willard.
Winchendon, ... Mr. Moses Hale.
Northbridge, ... Capt. Josiah Wood.
Ward, ... Mr. Joseph Stone.
Athol, ... Mr. Josiah Goddard.
Milford, ... Mr. David Stearns.
Sterling, ... Capt. Ephraim Wilder.
Boylston, ... Mr. Jonas Temple.

COUNTY OF CUMBERLAND.[3]

Falmouth, ... Daniel Ilsley, Esq.
                       John K. Smith, Esq.
Portland, ... Mr. John Fox.
Portland, ... Capt. Joseph McLellan.
North Yarmouth, . . David Mitchell, Esq.

[3][In the present State of Maine.]

Scarborough, ... William Thompson, Esq.
Brunswick, ... Capt. John Dunlap.
Harpswell, ... Capt. Isaac Snow.
Cape Elizabeth, . . . Mr. Joshua Dyer.
Gorham, ... Mr. Stephen Longfellow, Jr.
New Gloucester, . . . Mr. William Wedgery.
Gray, ... Rev. Samuel Perley.
Windham, ...
Standish, ...
Royalsborough, . . .
Raymondstown, . . .
Bakerstown, ...
Sylvester, ...
Bridgtown, ...
Shepardstown, . . .

COUNTY OF LINCOLN.[4]

Pownalborough, . . . Thomas Rice, Esq.
                        Mr. David Sylvester.
Georgetown, ... Mr. Nathaniel Wyman.
Newcastle, ... Mr. David Murray.
Woolwich, ... Mr. David Gilmore.
Waldoborough, . . .
Topsham, ... Hon. Samuel Thompson, Esq.
Winslow, ... Mr. Jonah Crosby.
Bowdoinham, . . . Mr. Zacheus Beal.
Boothbay, ... William McCobb, Esq.
Vassalborough, . . . Capt. Samuel Grant.
Bristol, ... William Jones, Esq.
Edgcomb, ... Moses Davis, Esq.
Hallowell, ... Capt. James Carr.
St. George's, ...
Warren, ...
Thomaston, ... David Fales, Esq.
Bath, ... Dummer Sewall, Esq.
Winthrop, ... Mr. Joshua Bean.
Lewistown, ...

[4][In the present State of Maine.]

Ballstown, ...
Walpole, ...
Wales, ...
Canaan, ...
Pittston, ...
Medumcook, ...
Norridgwalk, ...
Sterlington, ...
Belfast, ...
Machias, ...
Camden, ...
Hancock, ...

COUNTY OF BERKSHIRE.

Sheffield and }
Mt. Washington, } . . John Ashley, Jr., Esq.
Great Barrington, . . Hon. Elijah Dwight, Esq.
Stockbridge, ... Hon. Theodore Sedgwick, Esq.
Pittsfield, ... Capt. David Bush.
Richmond, ... Mr. Valentine Rathbun.
 Mr. Comstock Betts.
Lenox, ... Mr. Lemuel Collins.
Lanesborough, . . . Hon. Jonathan Smith, Esq.
Williamstown, . . . Hon. Tompson J. Skinner, Esq.
Adams, ... Capt. Jeremiah Pierce.
Egremont, ... Ephraim Fitch, Esq.
Becket, ... Mr. Elisha Carpenter.
West Stockbridge, . . Maj. Thomas Lusk.
Dalton, ...
Alford, ... Mr. John Hurlbert.
New Ashford, . . .
New Marlborough, . . Capt. Daniel Taylor.
Tyringham, ... Capt. Ezekiel Herrick.
Loudon, ... Mr. Joshua Lawton.
Windsor, ... Mr. Timothy Mason.
Partridgefield, . . . Ebenezer Peirce, Esq.
Hancock, ... Mr. David Vaughan.
Lee, ... Capt. Jesse Bradley.
Washington, ... Mr. Zenos Noble.
Sandisfield, ... Mr. John Picket, Jr.

Suggested Reading

Beard, Charles, *An Economic Interpretation of the Constitution*. New York: 1913.

Berns, Walter, *The Writing of the Constitution of the United States*. Washington: 1985.

Billias, George, *Elbridge Gerry: Founding Father and Republican Statesman*. New York: 1976.

Bloom, Sol, *The Story of the Constitution*. Washington: 1986.

Bowen, Catherine Drinker, *Miracle at Philadelphia*. Boston: 1966; 1986.

Bradford, M. E., *A Worthy Company: Brief Lives of the Framers of the United States Constitution*. Marlborough, N.H.: 1983.

Collier, James L., and Christopher Collier, *Decision in Philadelphia: The Constitutional Convention of 1787*. New York: 1985.

Corwin, Edward S., *The "Higher Law": Background of American Constitutional Law*. Ithaca, N.Y.: 1955.

Cullop, Floyd G., *The Constitution of the United States: An Introduction*. New York: 1984.

Farrand, Max, *The Framing of the Constitution of the United States*. New Haven: 1913.

Fiske, John, *The Critical Period in American History*. Boston: 1916.

Fowler, William M., Jr., *The Baron of Beacon Hill: A Biography of John Hancock*. Boston: 1980.

Friendly, Fred W., and Martha J. H. Elliot, *The Constitution. That Delicate Balance*. Washington: 1985.

Furtwangler, Albert, *American Silhouettes: Rhetorical Identities of the Founders*. New Haven: Yale University Press, 1987.

Hall, Van Beck, *Politics without Parties: Massachusetts, 1780-1791*. Pittsburgh: 1972.

Harding, Samuel B., *The Contest Over Ratification of the Federal Constitution in the State of Massachusetts*. Cambridge, Mass.: 1896.

Hayer, F. A., *The Constitution of Liberty*. Chicago: 1960.

Holcombe, Arthur N., *Our More Perfect Union*. Cambridge, Mass.: 1950.

Horton, James O., and Lois E. Horton, *Black Bostonians*. New York: Holmes & Meier, 1979.

112 Suggested Reading

Kammen, Michael, *A Machine that Would Go of Itself: The Constitution in American Culture*. New York: 1986.

Kelly, Alfred H., Winfred A. Harbison, and Herman Belz, *The American Constitution*. 6th ed., New York: 1983.

Kerber, Linda K., *Women of the Republic: Intellect and Ideology in Revolutionary America*. Chapel Hill: 1980.

Levy, Leonard, ed., *Essays on the Making of the Constitution*. 2nd ed., New York: 1982.

Main, Jackson Turner, *The Anti-Federalists: Critics of the Constitution, 1781-1788*. New York: 1961.

McDonald, Forrest, *Novus Ordo Seclorum: The Intellectual Origins of the Constitution*. Lawrence, Kansas: 1985.

McDonald, Forrest, *We the People: The Economic Origins of the Constitution*. Chicago: 1975.

McKenna, George, *A Guide to the Constitution: That Delicate Balance*. New York: 1984.

McLaughlin, Andrew C., *The Confederation and the Constitution, 1783-1789*. New York: 1967.

Mee, Charles L., Jr., *The Genius of the People*. New York: Harper & Row, 1987.

Norton, Mary Beth, *Liberty's Daughters: The Revolutionary Experience of American Women, 1750-1800*. Boston: 1980.

Peters, William. *A More Perfect Union*. New York: Crown Publishers, 1987.

Pinckney, Helen, *Christopher Gore: Federalist of Massachusetts, 1758-1827*. Waltham, Mass.: 1969.

Pyle, Christopher H., and Richard M. Pious, *The President, Congress, and the Constitution*. New York: 1984.

Rossiter, Clinton, *1787: The Grand Convention*. New York: 1966.

Van Doren, Carl, *The Great Rehearsal*. New York: 1969.

Warren, Charles, *The Making of the Constitution*. New York: 1967.

Wood, Gordon, *The Creation of the American Republic, 1776-1787*. New York: 1969.

Index

A

Active, James Turner, 2
Adams, John, 2, 15
Adams, Samuel, 13, 22 (illus.), 23, 32,
  47, 57, 59
Agriculture, 39, 41, 47
"Agrippa" (penname), 18
Alexandria, Virginia, 3
Amendments, 20-24, 55, 58-63, 65
American Revolution, 1, 3-4, 7, 15, 20,
  35, 44, 54
Ames, Fisher, 27
Anarchy, 23
Annapolis Convention, 3
Annapolis, Maryland, 4
Antifederalists, 11, 15-21, 23-24, 26,
  33, 35, 46, 50, 59
Areopagus, 53
Army and navy, 43-45, 56
Articles of Confederation, 3-4, 18, 27,
  37-39, 41, 45, 61, 64
Athenians, 53
Avery, John, 11

B

Barnstable, Massachusetts, 15
Barrell, Nathaniel, 23-24
Belknap, Rev. Jeremy, 12 (illus.), 17,
  19-20, 37
Berkshire County, 33, 46
Bill of Rights, 11, 18, 45, 55, 60
Bishop, Phaneul, 35
Boston, 1-2 (illus.), 4, 11-13, 24, 31, 33,
  39, 55, 59, 67-70
Boston Common, 31, 70
Bowdoin, James, Jr., 23

Bowdoin, Gov. James, 5-6, 13, 27-29
Brattle Street Church, 12
Bristol County, 47
British, 4
Brooks, Gen. John, 27, 29
Bunker Hill, 29

C

Cambridge, Massachusetts, 38
Charlestown, Massachusetts, 7, 13, 55
Chesapeake Bay, 3
China, 40
Commerce, 2-4, 7, 11, 14, 39-42, 45,
  56, 58, 62
Committee of Tradesmen, 70
Congress, 4, 10, 18, 20, 22, 26-27, 33-
  37, 39-46, 48, 50, 52, 55-58
Connecticut Compromise, 9
Constitution, Massachusetts, 9, 47, 53,
  55
Constitution (ship replica), 69
Constitution, U.S., 10-11, 13-21, 23-26,
  31-38, 42, 45-49, 51-57, 60-61, 63-65,
  67-68
Continental Army, 16
Continental Congress, 6-7, 21
Corsica, mortgaged to Genoese mer-
  chants, 41
Courts, 11. See also *Trial*
Currency, 4, 19, 37, 39, 62

D

Dana, Francis, 38
Dawes, Thomas, Jr., 39, 53-54
Debtors, 4, 6, 46
Declaration of Independence, 21

Dedham, Massachusetts, 27
Defense, 43-44, 56, 65
Delaware, 4
Democracy, compared to volcano, 27
Dictators of Rome, 31
Dorchester, Massachusetts, 13, 23
Douglas, Massachusetts, 19, 26
Duties on imports, 39-41, 46

E

Economy, 1-2, 4, 8, 17, 19, 39
Elections
    annual, 26-33
    biennial, 27-30, 32
    regulation of, 21, 33, 35-36
    septennial, 30, 32
    triennial, 30, 32
England, 30-31, 35, 40, 45, 58
Epistates of Athens, 31
Europe, 41

F

Faneuil Hall, 68 (illus.), 70
Farmers, 4-6, 14, 19, 39, 46-48
"Federal Constitution," good ship. See
    Constitution (ship replica)
Federal Street, 70
Federalists, 11, 14, 16-20, 23, 26-27, 29-
    30, 34, 36, 38-39, 49, 59-60, 69

G

General Court of Massachusetts, 5, 7-
    8, 10-11, 19, 30, 35, 44, 46, 55, 64
Georgia, 18, 44
Gerry, Elbridge, 9-10 (illus.), 11, 18-19
Gore, Christopher, 27, 31, 42, 52
Gorham, Nathaniel, 6-7 (illus.), 16, 55
Government, centralized, 3-8, 10, 14,
    20, 25
Government, locally autonomous, 9-11
Grand Procession, parade celebrating
    ratification, 68, 70
Great Britain, 1, 8, 14, 30, 41-43, 45-
    46

H

Hamilton, Alexander, 4, 69
Hampshire County, 9
Hancock family, 12
Hancock, Gov. John, 11, 13, 20-21 (il-
    lus.), 22-24, 29, 42, 55, 57-59, 62, 64
Harvard College, 8, 10, 18
Heath, Gen. William, 29, 49
Heavenly bodies, revolution of (anal-
    ogy), 29
Holmes, Abraham, 50, 52-53
House of Commons, 42
House of Representatives, 10, 26-27,
    31-33, 37-38

I

Imports. See *Duties on imports*
Indians, 2
Individualism, 3
Inquisition, Spanish, 52

J

Jarvis, Dr. Charles, 23, 59
Jefferson, Thomas, 2
John, King of England, 31
Johnson, Captain of artillery com-
    pany, 70
Jonah (biblical analogy), 20, 46
Judiciary, federal, 26, 50-51, 53-54
Jury. See *Trial*

K

King, Rufus, 7-8 (illus.), 16
Kinsley, Mr., 47
Knox, Gen. Henry, 16

L

Lanesborough, Massachusetts, 46
Leviathan, 20, 46
Lincoln, Gen. Benjamin, 6
Long Lane, 70
Long Lane house of worship, ii (fron-
    tis.), 12
Long Wharf, 2

M

Madison, James, 16
Maine, 14, 16, 26, 35, 44, 49
Manufactures, 39, 41
Marblehead, Massachusetts, 10-11
Maryland, 3-5, 8
Mason, George, 11
Massachusetts Bank, 39
Massachusetts Centinel, 19, 25, 67, 70
Massachusetts Gazette, 18, 25
Massachusetts Historical Society, 12
Medford, Massachusetts, 29
Money. See *Currency*
Montague, Admiral, 54
Montesquieu, 29, 31-32
Mount Vernon, 3
Mount Vernon Conference, 3

N

Nasson, Samuel, 19
Nationalism. See *Government, centralized*
Navigation rights, 3
Neal, James, 49
Negros, 49
New Gloucester, Maine, 19
New Hampshire, 12, 58
New Jersey, 4
New York, 4, 8, 58
Newburyport, Massachusetts, 8, 16, 35, 57
Nickerson the pirate, 54
North End, 13
Northampton, Massachusetts, 9
Norton, Massachusetts, 24, 34, 42

O

"Old Confederation," old ship of state, 69, 71
Old Revolutionaries, 14
Otis family, 15

P

Parliament, 30-32, 42, 45
Partridgefield, Massachusetts, 33
"Peculiar Institution." See *Slavery*

Pennsylvania, 4, 58
Philadelphia, 4, 6, 10-11, 16, 34
Philadelphia Convention, 6-11, 22, 38, 49-50, 54-55
Pierce, Ebenezer, 33
Pillars of government, 25 (illus.)
Pitt, Mr., 44
Plymouth County, 50
Potomac River, 3
Power, abuse of, 18, 36-37, 48, 53-54
Privateer, 35, 37
Puritans, 1

Q

Quaker, 49

R

Randolph, Edmund, 11
Ratification, 14, 16, 19, 21, 26, 49-50, 57, 60, 64, 67-69
Ratifying convention, Massachusetts, 11, 14, 16-18, 22-26, 45-46, 55-59, 61, 63-65, 67, 70
Rehoboth, Massachusetts, 35
Representation, 37-39, 43, 56-57. See also *Elections*
Republic and Republicanism, 1-3, 6, 18, 20, 22, 26, 50
Republican Volunteers, 70
Revolutionary Army, 6
Rhode Island, 4, 6, 58
Rochester, Massachusetts, 50, 53
Roxbury, Massachusetts, 13, 49

S

Sanford, Maine, 19
Saratoga, 29
Scarborough, Maine, 8, 19
Scituate, Massachusetts, 24, 29, 35
Senate, 32-33, 39, 43
Shattuck, Job, 5 (illus.)
Shays, Daniel, 5 (illus.), 6
Shays' Rebellion, 4-5, 9, 14, 17, 19, 29-30, 46-47
Shepherd, Gen. William, 6
Shipping, 40-41, 62

Singletary, Amos, 19, 46, 48
Slavery, 26, 49-50
Smallpox, 34
Smith, Jonathan, 46
South Carolina, 58
South End, 13
Spain, 52
Springfield, Massachusetts, 5-6
State House, Old, 1, 12, 67, 70
States' Rights, 9-11
Strong, Caleb, 9 (illus.), 10, 34
Supreme Court, Massachusetts, 5-6
Supreme Court, U.S., 53-54, 56
Sutton, Massachusetts, 19

T

Taxes, 5, 11, 21, 29, 39-40, 42-43, 45-46, 56
Taylor, Dr. John, 19, 23, 26-27, 37-38, 59
Terms for Congress, 26
Thompson, Gen. Samuel, 26, 29-30, 44, 49
Thompson, William, 19
Titles from foreign governments, 21
Topsham, Maine, 44
Trade. See *Commerce*
Treaties, 58

Trial: counsel, jury, witnesses, accusers, 51-57
Turner, Charles, 24, 29, 35, 61

V

Vermont, 6
Virginia, 3-4, 11, 58
Virginia Plan, 8
Volcano (analogy for democracy), 27

W

Waltham, Massachusetts, 31
War, declaration of, 43-44
Warren, James, 15
Warren, John, 1
Warren, Mercy Otis, 14-15 (illus.)
Washington, George, 3, 16, 49
Wedgery, William, 19, 24, 35, 47, 59
Whale (biblical analogy), 20, 46
White, Abraham, 24
White Plains, 29
William III, 32
Winthrop, James, 18
Worcester, Massachusetts, 4, 6

Y

York, Maine, 23

About the Authors

THOMAS H. O'CONNOR is a native of Boston, and a graduate of the Boston Latin School. After serving in the United States Army, he graduated from Boston College and received his Ph.D. from Boston University. Currently Professor of History at Boston College, Dr. O'Connor has written extensively about the Age of Jackson, the Civil War, and the history of Boston. He was named by President Ronald Reagan as a member of the Commission on the Bicentennial of the United States Constitution.

ALAN ROGERS was born in New England and educated in California. A specialist in the American Revolution and the Constitution, he joined the Department of History at Boston College in 1974. He is the author of several books and is currently working on studies of two Bostonians — a 19th century merchant seaman and a 20th century Federal District Court judge. Professor Rogers was named to the Boston Commission on the Bicentennial of the Constitution by Mayor Raymond L. Flynn.

WITHDRAWN
No longer the property of the
Boston Public Library.
Sale of this material benefits the Library.